The Power and the Glory

The Power and the Glory

The Authority of Jesus

JAMES JONES

DARTON · LONGMAN + TODD

First published 1994 by
Darton, Longman and Todd Ltd
1 Spencer Court
140–142 Wandsworth High Street
London SW18 4JJ

© 1994 James Jones

ISBN 0–232–52030–5

A catalogue record for this book is available
from the British Library

Scripture quotations are taken from
The Holy Bible, New International Version,
© 1973, 1978, 1984 by International Bible Society

Phototypeset by Intype, London
Printed and bound in Great Britain
at the University Press, Cambridge

To
Sarah
who has taught me more than any what it
means to follow the Lord Jesus

Contents

Author's Note

This book began life as a sermon series. It grew through being the substance of talks that I gave at several parish weekends for other churches. Most notably it took shape at the 1993 Swanwick Conference for Interserve, where I led the Bible readings on 'Jesus: The Power and the Glory'. At each stage I have benefited from the insights and questions of many people. I offer it now in published form as part of the ongoing discussion within the Church as to what it might mean for us to live under the authority of Jesus today.

I would like to acknowledge here the debt I owe to the reverend team of Sara Goatcher, Simon Oberst and David Richardson. I wish also to thank Mrs Pat Fox who with humour and patience has cracked the code and deciphered my illegible hand-writing.

My wife, Sarah, and my three children, Harriet, Jemima and Tabitha, are my great encouragers even though time spent on conferences and in my study inevitably has meant time away from them.

Preface

The writers of the New Testament all had an experience of Jesus. For some that experience was physical. John's first letter writes eloquently about that 'which we have heard, which we have seen with our eyes, which we have looked at and our hands have touched'. His experience of Jesus was tangible, visible and audible. For others, like Paul, the encounter with Jesus was after his death, when, on the Damascus Road, he heard a voice which identified itself as that of Jesus of Nazareth. Paul saw only a bright light. There was no physical contact. We might well describe his encounter as a spiritual experience.

It was out of the physical and spiritual experiences of Jesus, and upon them, that the New Testament writers constructed their theories about the identity of Jesus. The importance of identifying these origins lies in recognizing that it is 'experience' which characterizes our own spiritual life whether it is through reading the Bible, hearing it expounded, worship, the sacraments, prayer or meditation. These are the means whereby we expect to draw close to God through Jesus. Experience is the common ground between us and the New Testament writers.

This book is written out of the conviction that the more we can unearth the primary experiences of Jesus the clearer will be our own understanding of the identity of Jesus and what we can expect in our own spiritual encounters with him today.

The starting point I have chosen is the opening passage of the letter to the Hebrews. There is no evidence that the writer ever encountered Jesus in the flesh. It was clearly written many years after his death and resurrection. It reveals a high view of Jesus and lists seven extraordinary characteristics about him. He is:

> the heir to the universe
> the agent of creation
> the very light of God
> the image of God
> the sustainer of the cosmos
> the universal provider
> the ruler of heaven.

These seven features of Jesus Christ provide us with a Christology that is awesome in its scope. Given the interval of time between the death of Jesus and the presumed dating of this letter (c. AD 60) you could be forgiven for thinking that there had been some romantic gloss, some touching up of the icon.

Although the writers of the Gospels completed their work no earlier than the author of the letter to the Hebrews, they offer us a different style of literature. They narrate incidents from the life of Jesus and through these selected episodes serve us with their own interpretation of the identity of Jesus. Although the gospel writers have their own agenda, their own personality, their own readership through which the events of Jesus' life are filtered, they all present Jesus as a person of authority.

It is an authority the source of which Jesus was not, according to Luke, willing to disclose to his critics (Luke 20:8). But that authority was evident to eye-witnesses through what he said and did and how he behaved. There are nine specific episodes in the Gospels that explicitly refer to the authority of Jesus. These nine 'authorities' are as breathtaking in their scope as are the seven characteristics in the opening passage of Hebrews. Jesus has authority:

> to judge (John 5)
> to forgive (Mark 2)
> to overcome evil (Mark 3)

to heal (Matthew 10).
to lay down his life and take it up again (John 10)
to give life (Matthew 7)
to make disciples (Matthew 28).

What is significant is that each Gospel projects Jesus as a person with the authority to do certain things. It was through the *actions* of Jesus that his identity was revealed. It was as people encountered Jesus authoritatively doing certain things for them that they began to build up a picture of who he was. Although each of the writers, by the time they had come to write, had concluded that Jesus was the Christ, the Son of God, they all produced a narrative in which the key players made their discoveries about Jesus through experiencing what he did for them and to them.

Each chapter will look in detail at these different episodes, to explore the background to and the significance of what the writers have recorded about Jesus. But the aim will not be to leave us in the past but to show how their first experiences of Jesus can provide a model for our own experience of Jesus today. It is through concentrating on these passages of the New Testament that we shall also experience the authority of the Bible itself, for its unique exposition of the person of Jesus is the only substantial basis we have for evaluating our contemporary Christian experiences.

It may seem to be 'jumping the gun' to start with the systematic Christology of the letter to the Hebrews, yet the opening sentences give us one of the most succinct and yet grandest statements about Jesus in the whole of the New Testament. It shows where one particular Christian community had reached in their own appreciation of Jesus by the second half of the first century AD. Hopefully, by holding this theological work of art up to the light it will capture our hearts and minds and send us on a journey to discover the source of the artist's inspiration.

1

Jesus, The Character of God

In the past God spoke to our forefathers through the prophets at many times and in various ways, but in these last days he has spoken to us by his Son, whom he appointed heir of all things, and through whom he made the universe.

The Son is the radiance of God's glory and the exact representation of his being, sustaining all things by his powerful word. After he had provided purification for sins, he sat down at the right hand of the Majesty in heaven.

(Hebrews 1:1–3)

God has spoken

Christian theology and spirituality have their beginnings in the decisive act of God to reveal himself. Yet the spiritual encounter between God and ourselves is more often than not expressed in terms such as exploration, search, quest and discovery.[1]

These words stress the part played by us in the spiritual experience. But if they are over-emphasized they misrepresent the Christian faith as a religion of discovery whereby men and women, out of the core of their being, simply do their best to find what lies at the hub of the universe and to make any connection they can. There is of course much in the Bible that echoes this quest and exploration, not least the search for meaning and love throughout the Psalms:

As the deer pants for streams of water,
  so my soul pants for you, O God.
My soul thirsts for God, for the living God.
  When can I go and meet with God? (Psalm 42)

There is also much in our contemporary culture that makes it
more comfortable for Christians to talk about their faith as a
quest. Everybody is embarked upon their own journey. We are
all fellow travellers. Each of us makes our own discoveries. In
such a climate nobody is wrong or right and all pursue the
vision that they themselves see. The democratic ethos and the
philosophical need for relativism – where everybody does what
is right in their own eyes – create an atmosphere in which
Christians can breathe easily and talk about their faith in purely
personal terms, as a private experience in which they have made
certain discoveries about the world and themselves. But
although the Christian faith has always welcomed the adventur-
ous seeker after God and yielded countless discoveries to the
spiritual explorer, it would not be fair to its original and essential character to leave it at that. From the beginning it has been a
religion of revelation. And there is a world of difference
between revelation and discovery; it is the difference between
going into a darkened room and groping to find the light, and
entering the same room with someone directing you to the
switch. Discovery is not the same as revelation. They are two
different activities. In the sphere of religion they speak of
initiatives – one human, the other divine.

The statement 'God has spoken' underlines the divine initiative at the heart of the Christian faith and emphasizes its character as a religion of revelation. From Genesis to the Book of
Revelation this is God being God when he speaks and com-
municates. It is his nature to do so. Anyone who has any inkling
that at the source of the universe is a God of love should surely
not be surprised to learn that the one who is committed to
perfect communion with his creation is constantly expressing
himself and communicating to that end. Love issues in

communication and communion. Love involves self-disclosure, for how else can there be communion? Love is therefore a commitment to self-revelation. And that is why the Christian faith, whose central text is 'God so loved the world . . .', is necessarily and essentially a religion not of discovery but of revelation.

Those who play down the notion of divine revelation and over-emphasize the role of human discovery in the Christian faith are unwittingly undermining the one doctrine that unites all Christians: namely, that God loves the world.

It makes little sense to talk about a God of love at the heart of the universe standing, as it were, with his arms folded, lips sealed, leaving everybody else to do the running. Such a mute and unyielding character hardly rates as a God of love. If a loving God stands at the centre of the universe then it is entirely consistent with this view that he should communicate with the end of entering into communion with those he loves. That communication necessarily involves him in self-disclosure and personal revelation, for how else can his beloved know who they are to relate to? The theology that God is Love is the very foundation of the doctrine of revelation. Love involves self-disclosure and is therefore a commitment to revelation.

It is that essence of revelation which the author of the letter to the Hebrews captures when he writes unequivocally: 'In the past God spoke . . . in the last days he has spoken to us by a son.' The Jewish religion maintained a strong tradition of God speaking to them through the prophets. This latest mouthpiece of God is seen here not just as a prophet but in terms of a much more intimate relationship with God, as a son.

The prophets were spiritual people, often noble and courageous, but in spite of their virtues were as clay-footed as the rest of humanity. While men and women reached out in search of the true way to live, what came to them through these devout people were reminders about God's judgement and mercy, and parables and propositions as to how they should conduct themselves.

Eventually God answered the human quest for truth not with a set of abstract moral propositions but by presenting the world with a True person untrammelled by the flaws of human nature. This Son was as much a disclosure of the character of God as he was the epitome of a perfect human being. He was not just God's mouthpiece as were the prophets, he was God's son personally expressing God's love to the world. He was the messenger and the message itself.

Of course all this was not immediately evident. These conclusions were drawn after much reflection on the encounters with Jesus. But the point is that these ideas are consistent with the general human intuition that if at the centre of the universe there stands a God of love, then you would expect him to reveal himself in such a way that we could know and reciprocate that love.

On one level it still seems extraordinary that a Palestinian craftsman, living two thousand years ago, could be the one through whom God made the universe and be the exact representation of his being. On another level, it is entirely appropriate that the God of love should disclose the secrets of his heart to those he loves, and that this expression should find its fullest revelation not just in words spoken or written but in the tangible, audible and visible dimensions of a human being.

If Christianity were solely a religion of discovery then it would be like a game without known rules, in which all the players simply look for clues as to how they should play it. As it is, the Christian faith was born out of the decisive and loving act of God to reveal himself. He made himself as accessible as he could to the human family, 'he spoke to us by a son', – flesh to flesh, spirit to spirit, person to person.

'The Son is the radiance of God's glory'

This phrase conjures up a picture of brightness radiating from a source of pure light. It is an image which the Gospel of John also applies to Jesus: 'I am the light of the world.' Yet so often our interpretation of this picture is conditioned by our own environment and is therefore limited. Lights in the modern world are strong and bright and harsh on the eye. These are the powerful lamps of theatres and television studios. Household lights are not the sort that you would look at when switched on. Even hand-held torches are too bright to look at for any length of time. These lights are for dispelling the darkness and for illumining stages, sets, rooms and paths. Consequently, wherever we come across the symbol of light in the Christian faith we interpret it almost always in terms of what the light illumines as it sheds its rays across the darkness. Whenever the Gospels imagine Jesus as the light of the world we think of the dispelling of darkness, the exposing of sin, the lighting up of the way of truth. All these interpretations have integrity with the text.

But there is another aspect to Jesus being like light that is often overlooked because of our own particular experience of electric light which, of course, was unseen in first century Palestine. Light in the time of Jesus came from waxed tapers and oil lamps. The flickering flames that danced in the darkness were moving pictures that invited you to stare, to meditate, to dream and imagine in the same way that we might sit entranced before a log fire. Here was a light that did not turn your head away through its harsh brightness but invited you to look again and again at the flame and its source.

John records Jesus as saying: 'When a person looks at me, they see the one who sent me. I have come as light into the world so that no one who believes in me should stay in darkness' (John 12:45, 46). Here he is making this double interpretation of light. Jesus, the light of the world, not only dispels the darkness but illumines the very source of light so that whoever looks lingeringly at Jesus, the light, will see more clearly the one who sent him into the world.

As the radiance of God's glory, Jesus invites us to focus on him not to be blinded but to see more fully the nature of God who is the ground, the source of his own being. To meditate on

Jesus, the light, is like looking through the yellow-orange flame of a coal fire into the white heat at the heart of the glowing embers. There is no flame without the fire, as Augustine reminded us. They belong together. The flame is the fire's radiance.

Jesus is the radiance of God's glory. To listen to his judgements is to be brought face to face with God's passion for justice. To hear his pronouncements of forgiveness is to experience the absolution of God's compassion. To witness his authority over the demonic is to see God's pledge to banish evil from his creation. To watch the sick made well at his touch is to be reminded of God's promise to make all things new. To behold him laying down his life is to stand in awe of the sacrifice and self-giving of God that stands at the heart of the universe. To see the spiritually dead come alive through their encounters with him is to observe that transfusion of life eternal that only God can give. To sit at the feet of this teacher is to be caught up in God's own commitment to all that is true. To be made one of his disciples is to learn that God is without frontiers in his seeking out of the lost. Jesus is the flame of God's fire. He is the radiance of God's glory. To come near to him is to come closer to God himself and to be warmed by the burning fire, as St Paul wrote:

> For God, who said, 'Let light shine out of darkness', made his light shine in our hearts to give us the light of the knowledge of the glory of God in the face of Christ. (2 Corinthians 4:6)

'The exact representation of his being'

Being the son of a carpenter Jesus was no stranger to those who crafted with wood, be it the making of a simple bowl or the painstaking engraving of furniture. The Greeks had a word for the tool used to engrave – 'character' which became also a metaphor meaning 'stamp' or 'imprint'. Interestingly, this word occurs only once in the whole of the New Testament. In the opening passage of Hebrews it is used to describe Jesus as 'the exact representation' of the being of God. Jesus is the being of God engraved in flesh and blood. It is not just that Jesus shows us the character of God. He *is* God's character, the divine *engravure* in human flesh.

When people make impressions of ancient brasses they cover the figure with paper and rub over it with waxed crayon. The image of the now covered and invisible brass comes through in the different substance of the paper and crayon. In a similar way the image of the veiled and invisible God comes through to us in the different substance of the flesh and blood of Jesus of Nazareth. Here is God's character for all eyes to see.

Jesus came on to the world's stage not just to tell us about God and so help us in our search. He came and showed us God. There is a world of difference between the two. It is not a perfect analogy (analogies never are) but it is the difference between biography and autobiography. In the former, a well-researched writer tells us all he knows about the subject he has studied. He shares with us the discoveries that he has made. He interprets the significance of the events in the life of his subject. In the latter, the autobiography reveals the author. What he writes and, equally importantly, how he writes it express the author himself. It is his character in black and white. Biography is about discovery. Autobiography is self-expression, self-disclosure and self-revelation. (And even if in an autobiography there is dissembling and deceit and a glossing over the facts, then these things in themselves reveal the nature of the person who has written.) Jesus is God's character, the being of God written small enough for human eyes to see. Jesus of Nazareth is God writing about himself in flesh and blood. That is how the author of the letter to the Hebrews sees Jesus. As John Baillie succinctly summarized: 'He gives us himself in communion. God does not give us information about himself.'[2] He *is* the exact expression of God's being.

'Through whom he made the universe'

In spite of modern theological reflection on the doctrine of the Trinity, the average Christian still maintains a fundamental view of the three persons of the Godhead:

> God the Father made the world,
> God the Son saved the world, and
> God the Spirit renews the world.

Although each of the persons of the Trinity stands appropriately in the front line of each of these activities and, therefore, provides some grounds for differentiation among the three, the pages of Scripture suggest a much less clear-cut distinction. Here, for example, the writer to the monotheistic Hebrews identified Jesus as being fully involved in the creation of the world. The son is God's agent of creation. Strictly speaking he is described as the one through whom God 'made the worlds', but as the classicist and theologian F. F. Bruce comments: 'The whole created universe of space and time is meant.'[3] Certainly this accords with other primary chapters in the New Testament such as John 1 and Colossians 1 where we find 'all things were made through him; and without him was not anything made that was made' and 'all things have been created through him, and unto him'.

This high view of Jesus of Nazareth implicating him fully in the making of the universe is a challenge to the piety of all of us who claim a personal experience of Jesus. The focus or rather locus of that encounter is more often Calvary, than creation. The death of Jesus on the cross and the forgiveness that issues with the blood flowing from his wounds, the resurrection and the promise to be always with those who open their hearts to him – these are the opening chords of a new symphony for the believer. But, rather like a child learning to play the piano who instead of progressing through the more difficult sections of her piece keeps playing the familiar opening bars, so many

Christians who encounter Jesus at Calvary fail to pursue him into creation. Our myopic vision sees him at close quarters as Saviour but not in the distance as Creator. Such a limited view of Jesus has serious implications for it allows us to enjoy our faith as a private spiritual experience without fully appreciating the global repercussions of giving our allegiance to the one through whom God made the whole universe. A truly high view of Jesus should make Christians passionate about what happens in and to *his* creation.

'Sustaining all things by his powerful word'

If the idea of Jesus being the agent of God's creation came as a shock to the Hebrews, then this affirmation about the carpenter from Nazareth currently sustaining all things must surely have taken their breath away. Admittedly this letter was written decades after the death of Jesus but of all the writing in the New Testament it was addressed most explicitly to people of a Jewish background. The Jews, like Moslems today, were staunchly monotheistic. They saw God as Creator and Sustainer of the universe. For those two divine activities to be shared with and to be ascribed to the person of a carpenter from Nazareth must surely have taken a lot of believing.

Sometimes when we consider our own religious experience and compare it with those in the first century we can be misled into thinking that it was somehow easier for them to believe it all. They stood nearer to events in time. Even if they had not seen Jesus themselves there were still eye-witnesses who could testify to what they had heard. Furthermore, they did not have the advanced scientific understanding of the nature and complexity of the universe that we have. None of these points should ever be underestimated. However, they had their own obstacles to believing in Jesus, not least their own deeply rooted faith and world-view.

If today a person lays claim to being divine he is treated with amusement, as an eccentric. If he should persist with this view and become socially disruptive in the process he is committed to a psychiatric hospital. Our society, which is by and large apathetic to convictions about God, tolerates any number of extravagant religious claims. In the Jewish communities (of the first century) the culture was very different. For a human being to make himself out to be somehow equal with God was not an amusing indiscretion but an outrageous offence to the religious sensibilities of the whole community – the sort of thing that would have the crowds pushing you off a cliff (Luke 4:29) or stoning you (John 10:31). Jesus narrowly escaped both these fates. The monotheistic Jews took God much more seriously than we do. To impersonate God was an intolerable scandal. It not only shocked the devout it also threatened the religious fabric of the community which bound them together and gave them their identity.

Their history and the interpretation given to it by the Torah and the prophets gave to the Jewish people their sense of nationhood and purpose. In times of adversity, such as being invaded and occupied by a foreign power, the natural tendency was to hold on ever more securely to the traditions and religious insights of the past. First-century Palestine, occupied by the Roman Army, was not therefore the most opportune time for people to think in new and imaginative ways about God. Furthermore, maintaining scrupulously their traditions – such as keeping the Sabbath observance – was a way of reinforcing to themselves their own unique character in a country which was theirs but infested and ruled by a foreign presence. Indeed, G. B. Caird, the New Testament scholar, maintained that it was precisely for this reason that the Jewish leaders found it difficult to stomach the way Jesus so disregarded the Sabbath.[4] It was not just that he broke the religious rules, it was that by so doing he dealt a blow to the pride of a nation whose distinctive character was being maintained in adversity by the observance of such rules. He was not just a religious maniac but also a traitor.

The religious traditions were an integral part of the life of the

Jewish communities, not just for those in Palestine but also for those dispersed in foreign cultures along the eastern coast of the Mediterranean from Alexandria to Rome. For a Jew to believe that a human being could also be the Sustainer of the universe required a major shift in their outlook as unsettling as any volcanic eruption. In spite of all the prophecies about God sending a specially anointed servant into the world the resistance in the Jewish heart and mind to believing that one of their number – and in particular Jesus of Nazareth – could also be the Sustainer of the universe was much greater than the resistance we might feel to believing that the window cleaner was an angel sent from God.

It is the sheer extraordinariness of the claims made about Jesus that impel us to enquire, as we shall do in these pages, how in spite of all the cultural obstacles (let alone the vicious persecution that ensued from such a faith) so many Jews should have acquired the view and persisted with the belief that Jesus was the Sustainer of all things.

To see Jesus as such ascribes to him universal power. More often than not when we think of creation we see it in terms of a past event. In the creed, for instance, we declare our faith in God who made the world in the past tense. This conjures up a picture of some cosmic happening that belongs way back in the history of time. But the description of Jesus here suggests that his involvement with creation continues to this very moment in time. It is he who is supplying the energy for creation to continue.

A picture that comes to mind is of a child's spinning top. It can only stand and hum if there is a constant source of energy being supplied to it. Parents pump the handle vigorously so that the top spins and hums and delights the child. Just as the toy requires a constant supply of energy to do what it was intended to do, so creation too requires of God, the source of all power, the same supply of energy to fulfil its purpose. If God withdraws this vital force then all creation would implode like a shattering light bulb. The universe continues to hold together because of the giving of energy from God himself. It is in this sense that creation is every bit as much an act of grace as salvation. What is more, according to the writer to the Hebrews, it is Jesus, the author of our faith at Calvary, who stands at the centre of the universe as the author of the universe. Jesus is the source of both graces, creation and salvation. Both are his acts of grace. Furthermore, it means that creation has not stopped. The process of creation goes on as the Son sustains the universe with his power. Like a sculptor working with imperfect materials so the Son wrestles with the flaws in his creation. His watchword is 'Behold, I am making all things new'. He continues to make, to create until perfection is attained.

'He is appointed heir of all things'

Not only is the Son instrumental in the act of creation but as the letter to the Colossians underlines 'All things were created by him and for him' (1:16). This means that everything in creation, the visible and the invisible, the material and the spiritual are all dedicated to the Son.

Paul Avis[5] has identified two features of the New Age movement (although 'movement' may be too grand a word for the pot-pourri of religious ideas and practices that defy too tight a definition). He observes an ecological and a therapeutic dimension. In the former there is justifiable concern for the future of the environment, in the latter there is a preoccupation with well-ness and a myriad suggestions on finding the secret of spiritual, mental and physical well-being.

Very few people are left untouched by fears for the future of the planet. Damage to the delicate fabric of the universe and the knowledge of ever-dwindling resources present us with a scenario that is apocalyptic in its proportions. This, of course, provides us with a context for reading the letter to the Hebrews which is very different from that of the original audience. And yet it is to our situation that these words speak dramatically.

Most people's concern for the environment arises naturally out of the instinct to survive. But here we find another angle. For those with an allegiance to Jesus Christ there follows a commitment to the whole created order because it is for him and he is the heir of all things. To be concerned for the environment is therefore not just an inveterate act of obedience to the survival instinct but an act of homage to the one for whom the creation was destined. Words written two thousand years ago have in our lives assumed a greater relevance and a new urgency.

The Son's inheritance, of course, encompasses the material as well as the spiritual. Christians, however, need reminding of this because historically we have always subordinated the former to the latter. A legacy of the way the essence of the Christian faith was drained through the filter of other philosophies is that, against all the evidence of the Old Testament, the material order came to be seen as the enemy of the spiritual realm. Evidence of this is to be found in the Church's attitudes in the past to the body and sexuality and in the present to wealth and industry, and yet the emphasis of the Bible's opening chapter testified to the original goodness of the material world. Although the physical world of matter became the arena in which the human challenge to God's authority would be acted out, it nevertheless was and remains originally good. And as the letter to the Hebrews insists, it is still the Son's inheritance.

The dichotomy between spirit and matter is a serious problem for Christians today. Many, for example, find it difficult to make any fundamental connection between their faith and their work. Church is a place for nursing the wounds of work. It is a spiritual retreat from the world. There is little there that makes any connection between spirit and matter, faith and work, and which propels the believer back in to God's world. Vicars, like myself, conspire unwittingly to keep it like that. We concentrate on recruiting Youth leaders, Children's leaders, Housegroup leaders, Synod members and so give the impression that the most valued thing a person can do is the spiritual work of the Church! And should someone ever aspire to Ordained ministry then such a fuss is made of the person that it makes the celebration party for the prodigal's return look rather like the sharing of a bag of stale crisps on a wet afternoon! The message that we constantly give out is that it is the Church that is God's primary concern. It is of the utmost importance that the Church should be well-equipped for its mission, but there is the issue of balance: God loved the world so much, not just the Church, that he sent his Son. This Son is Lord not just of the Christian community but of all creation.

Over the years of being in the Ordained ministry I have made a point of spending days with different members of the congregation shadowing them in their place of work. It has taken me to such places as the offices of accountants, and of local government, into police cells with a criminal defence lawyer to those charged with rape and attempted murder, down into the excavated tunnels beneath the Channel, to the paperless open-plan offices of a computer company, and behind the scenes of a large international hotel. This exercise has done two things. Firstly, it has earthed my own ministry as a teacher in a parish church so that I might be more relevant in my exposition of the Christian faith and its relationship to God's world. Secondly, I hope that it affirms those I spend the time with, helping them to realize that they do their work as servants of God in a world that belongs to God and which is as much his concern as the Church. Faith and work belong together because both spirit and matter are the Son's inheritance. It is because the Son is 'the heir of *all* things' that we know that matter as well as spirit matters to God.

'After he had provided purification for sins'

The other feature of the New Age movement identified by Avis is its preoccupation with therapy and healing. There is a diagnosis and prescription of the dis-eased human condition that is uniquely Christian. Christianity is not the only religion in the world to point out the moral flaws that universally afflict the characters of human beings. The uniqueness of Jesus Christ lies in him being the only founder of a major world religion to be described and prescribed by his followers as purging away our sins, as cleansing and purifying us. What is suggested here in this passage explicitly is that an encounter with Jesus is a cathartic experience in which we find the forgiveness of sins and healing. This catharsis is the therapy that God offers through his Son to those in search of peace and wellness.

When Luke records the angels announcing the birth of Jesus he gives the reason for rejoicing: 'For unto you is born this day in the city of David a Saviour (a Forgiver).' They did not announce the arrival of an economist or even an environmentalist – although two thousand years on, judging from the media, you would imagine that is where our salvation lay. We certainly at this moment in time would benefit greatly from both sound economists and good environmentalists. But two thousand years ago and ever since, right up until this present day and beyond, our radical human need has been to find someone to heal the sores of our souls and the carcinomas of our conscience. Finding forgiveness through an encounter with Jesus has been a constant and central theme of Christian experience down the ages. The Bible proclaims it, the liturgies celebrate it. The letter to the Hebrews dwells on it in exquisite detail. It was to this end that God sent his Son into the world. The secret of his mission was in the meaning of his name, Jesus: God saves. His coming was the act of someone in love with those he had made and, in spite of their restlessness and intransigence, committed to their eternal well-being. It is time for us to look more closely at the accounts of those who experienced him in the flesh. It is time to leave the mountains and this high view of Jesus and to walk the foothills of Judea in the footsteps of those who met him face to face.

2

The Authority of Jesus to Judge

So, because Jesus was doing these things on the Sabbath, the Jews persecuted him. Jesus said to them: 'My Father is always at his work to this very day, and I, too, am working.' For this reason the Jews tried all the harder to kill him; not only was he breaking the Sabbath, but he was even calling God his own Father, making himself equal with God.

Jesus gave them this answer: 'I tell you the truth, the Son can do nothing by himself; he can do only what he sees his Father doing, because whatever the Father does the Son also does. For the Father loves the Son and shows him all he does. Yes, to your amazement he will show him even greater things than these. For just as the Father raises the dead and gives them life, even so the Son gives life to whom he is pleased to give it.

'Moreover, the Father judges no one, but has entrusted all judgement to the Son, that all may honour the Son just as they honour the Father. He who does not honour the Son does not honour the Father, who sent him.

'I tell you the truth, whoever hears my word and believes him who sent me has eternal life and will not be condemned; he has crossed over from death to life. I tell you the truth, a time is coming and has now come when the dead will hear the voice of the Son of God and those who hear will live. For as the Father has life in himself, so he has granted the Son to have life in himself. And he has given him authority to judge because he is the Son of Man.

'Do not be amazed at this, for a time is coming when all

who are in their graves will hear his voice and come out –
those who have done good will rise to live, and those who
have done evil will rise to be condemned. By myself I can do
nothing; I judge only as I hear, and my judgement is just, for
I seek not to please myself but him who sent me.

(John 5:16–30)

To begin with the concept of judgement is, I fear, the least appealing way to proceed! It's as appetizing as steak and kidney pie to a vegetarian. It is not a subject that warms the heart. And yet there it is, central to the teaching of Jesus. Judgement is seen so often in the same category as judgementalism which is a characteristic of many religious people. In a universe where we all feel increasingly insecure there is something comforting and reassuring in holding onto spiritual and moral absolutes. Wrapping ourselves in a duvet of warm certainty we feel safe from and more able to cope with the cold draughts of change and moral ambiguity. Although we find refuge in this place (and there's no doubt that both the Bible and the teaching of Jesus encourage us to rest here from time to time), it is not very long before the duvet has become a wall over which we can look with disapproval on those outside.

Christians can come across as censorious and judgemental in the areas of both personal morality and social justice. We hoist the standard, salute the flag and give the impression that those who are not with us are somehow inferior. The result is that the Church becomes a narrow and restrictive sect turned in on its righteous self rather than a community that is open and welcoming of those on its edges. Its preoccupation with defining standards, be they in the fields of sexual morality or international justice, gives it an unattractive and judgemental character that not only alienates the outsider but also suffocates some of its members, especially when they become aware of their own moral weakness.

By drawing attention to this problem I am not suggesting that there is no place for making judgements about how we should behave but simply acknowledging that by mounting the skate-board called 'judgement' we can very easily and very quickly career off in the disastrous direction of 'judgementalism'.

There is also a breed of people who are sticklers for the rules. They are impervious to reason. There can be no exceptions and no compromise. When you plead with them to make some allowance you notice they are dead behind the eyes. Some-thing's missing. Of course, 'right' is on their side. They are simply going by the rules. And it is more than their job's worth to deviate.

The worst of the Pharisees in the time of Jesus were very similar. They knew the law and its small print. They were meticulous in keeping the tiniest detail and in making sure that everybody else did too (Matthew 5:17–26). They were famous and infamous for doing so. And you can find such people today inside the Church. (There's usually an empty seat on either side of them in a meeting!)

Self-righteousness and judgementalism have always been an occupational hazard for religious people. It was an ugly feature of some of the Pharisees. That's why Jesus told them the funny line about those who try to get the sawdust out of a friend's eye while they've got a huge plank shooting out of their own (Matthew 7:1–6). This is the humour of the carpenter's work-shop! Imagine, if you had a wooden beam jutting out of your eye, long before you had got anywhere near your friend's speck you'd have poked his eye out with the plank! It was an hilarious scene. Jesus uses this comic sketch to warn religious people of the hypocrisy of judgementalism. At the risk of ruining the story (for to explain a parable can be as wearisome as trying to explain a joke) there's an aspect of the scene worth exploring. Both characters have a problem with something in their eye. The story would, on one level, work just as well if the man with the speck had had something wrong with his ear or his back. The fact that they both had the *same* problem to a greater or lesser degree underlines the point that the faults we see most easily and quickly in others are the very faults that we ourselves have, and often more acutely. I'm aware of this in my own relationships. I'm most critical (in my own thoughts) of people when they have failed in precisely those areas where, if I am honest, I know I am weakest. I will spare you the catalogue – but it's a worthwhile exercise to cast your mind back over recent episodes when you've been critical of others and ask yourself if these faults, which you have identified, are not a mirror of your own weaknesses and errors. It is precisely because we have these blemishes that we vent our frustration and self-criticism by transferring it to and piling it on those who are around us. The criticism that we mete out to others is rooted in a subconscious self-criticism. No wonder Jesus promised that 'in the same way as you judge others, you will be judged', for, in truth, we have already begun to pass judgement on ourselves by the way we judge others. Furthermore, we have judged them more severely because in so doing we can lighten our own burden of guilt. 'After all, we're not as bad as them!' Here is a root of judgementalism. It is a means of limiting our guilt and salvaging some self-respect. But, as we shall see in the next chapter, there is only one way to do that. Judgementalism is a feature of the religious person who has not yet experienced in the depth of his psyche the neutralizing effects of God's forgiveness and the self-acceptance that comes through the experience of being accepted by God.

I think this was the source of Jesus' challenge to the Pharisees. Given their prickly character and censorious judgements it may, at first, appear surprising that Jesus should tell his followers to make sure their 'righteousness surpasses that of the Pharisees and teachers of the Laws'. Did he want them to be even more pernickety and finicky than these religious nit-pickers?

Jesus made it clear that the law revealed in the Old Testament still stood. His followers were not to break it but to obey it. He allowed no wedge to be driven between the Old Testament and his own teaching. But keeping the law had to go beyond the legalism of these dead-behind-the-eyes Pharisees. What was missing from them was not judgement but compassion. In their insistence on justice they showed no mercy to those who failed. Nobody could have been more righteous than these teachers of the law. But the righteousness that surpassed that of the Pharisees was one which reached beyond itself to the gentle dew of mercy.

Christians should have a different manifesto from those who call for justice in society. We're committed to a kingdom not only of justice but of mercy. A society that is built on justice alone can be a very cruel place for sinners. Self-righteous people strutting around demanding everybody toe the line are a nightmare.

The Christian community is to be a model of righteousness and compassion. The essence of the kingdom of God is an amalgam of justice and mercy. It is mercy, personally experienced and publicly expressed, that protects a Christian community from being an introverted and judgemental sect.

Having declared that we must avoid the dangers of judgementalism we cannot avoid the implications of this chapter from John that the Evangelist clearly saw in the mission of Jesus strong elements of divine judgement. You don't have to be an astute observer to realize that the concept of divine judgement is one of the least fashionable doctrines in the Church today. It conjures up medieval paintings of God consigning hordes of writhing bodies to hideous torment. Such a picture does not fit with our modern understanding of God who, as the Bible says is 'slow to anger, abounding in love' (Psalm 103:8). It is felt that the judgemental character of God displayed in the Old Testament gives way to the compassionate nature revealed in Jesus. The Old Testament, it is said, reveals a God of judgement whereas the New Testament demonstrates a God of love. Judgement and love are seen as the antithesis of each other. They are mutually exclusive doctrines. Judgement means you are not loving; loving means you cannot judge.

The doctrine of divine judgement has also been eclipsed by the doctrine of universalism. This holds that all people will be saved. It is based upon the understanding that God's love is absolute and that his love will encompass even the most intransigent sinner. It is an optimistic doctrine expressing the faith that even the most evil and rebellious of God's detractors, will, when faced with the enormity of his mercy, capitulate in repentance and acceptance of his grace. This doctrine of universalism envisages a new world transformed under the absolute sway of God's love. Such a doctrine allows Christians to be very relaxed in their relationships with other faith communities and with those of little or no faith at all. It allows for open relationships of mutual listening and dialogue without the intrusion of any uncomfortable or exclusive claims about the founder of the Christian faith.

While I do not wish to trace over the medieval scenes of bodies tormented in a gruesome underworld, we cannot avoid this passage with its explicit references to the judgement of God. Although Jesus distances God the Father from the process of judgement ('The Father judges no one' v. 22) he does so in the same breath as implicating himself ('The Father has entrusted all judgement to the Son' v. 22). Although this quotation is lifted from the Gospel of John which was written later than the others, the theme of divine judgement weaves strongly through the earlier Gospels and the letters of Paul. The view that the Old and New Testaments can be distinguished on the grounds that the latter is free of Old Testament pictures of divine judgement does not square with a proper reading. There are over one hundred references to aspects of divine judgement in the New Testament. Moreover, the Evangelists not only record Jesus as the author of many warnings of the dangerous and impending judgement of God but also ascribe to Jesus the authority to be involved in the judging himself. The gospel writers who project Jesus as a person of deep compassion and furnish us with all that we know about the love-of-God-in-Jesus are precisely the same people who paint a picture of him as one given authority by the Father to judge. However much we may like to play 'pick a stick' with the texts of the Gospels we will find that as soon as we start picking out a verse about Jesus that tells of God's love we dislodge another stick that speaks of God's judgement.

Love and judgement do not in the New Testament appear to be such a paradox. To the modern mind they may appear as complete opposites, as expressed in the question: 'How can a God of love possibly judge people?' Love and judgement seem incompatible. But in the Bible – and, indeed, to the modern mind on reflection – love is not the opposite of judgement. The opposite of judgement is mercy. Love is the source of both. Love issues in both judgement and mercy.

When you love someone, you care about what happens to them. Wherever possible you try to protect them. You stand up for them. If you have the power to do it you take action – appropriate and proportionate – to stop the person getting hurt. Love takes steps to minimize evil. Such a move is an act of judgement. It involves discerning between right and wrong and taking action against that which is destructive. Its source lies in love. That is not to say that in the realm of human affairs these actions won't be sullied by the imperfections of human nature but it helps us to see that there is a link between the source of love and the activity of judgement.

This link is actually recognized in the other question that many ask: 'If there's a God of love why doesn't he do something about the state of the world?' Implicit in this question is the idea that love should not be totally passive but active in rescuing the oppressed, healing the wounded and in righting wrongs. What people are looking for in the name of love is not words but action. The God of love is being called upon to separate the good from the bad (the sheep from the goats, the wheat from the tares – to use some of Jesus' own imagery), to put an end to the maltreatment of the weak (the hungry, the thirsty, the stranger, the naked, the sick, the prisoner – to use more of Jesus' categories) and to establish a world where at last good triumphs over evil. This is the judgement implicit in the question. Its source is in the eternal spring of God's love. God's love propels him into executing judgement, setting his face against injustice and releasing the oppressed. There is an inextricable link between justice in human affairs and the judgement of God. It is a curious feature, therefore, of modern Christian thinking that while there has been a grand discovery of the biblical theme of justice there has been an embarrassed silence about the biblical theme of judgement.

For the prophets such as Isaiah and Amos and in the teachings of Jesus the two go hand-in-hand. In his love for the world God rightly sets his face against all that desecrates his creation; he reels back at the scale of human injustice; he pledges himself to the righting of wrongs and to the ultimate overthrowing of all evil influences; he impresses upon people through the prophets and Jesus the reality of this judgement; yet in his love he not only reels back in judgement but he also leans forward in mercy offering forgiveness to those of us who, in spite of our best intentions, have contributed to the sum of human sadness through our own selfishness.

God's love issues in both judgement and mercy. In the next chapter we shall look more closely at divine mercy. Here we simply recognize that mercy actually implies judgement and that the doctrine of God's love is the source of the doctrines of mercy and judgement. This is what we see and hear in the life and teachings of Jesus. This is no paradox. Love and judgement are consistent with each other. If my children are fighting and I intervene to stop them and to protect them from each other, I do this act of judgement as a father who loves them and wants the best for them. I would forfeit any right to be considered a caring parent if I let the stronger intimidate the weaker. It is love that demands both justice and judgement. Love requires that the world should be fair and takes steps to ensure that it should become so. Love is not just an aspiration for fairness, an abstract concept called justice, it is an active movement to overthrow evil, to release the oppressed, to right the wrongs: it is a loving act called judgement.

In the Bible this divine action of judgement is both present and future. Most Christians when thinking of God's judgement see it mainly as a future event. But there are at least two dimensions of divine judgement being experienced in the present.

One way in which God acts against evil and selfishness is to expose it for what it is in the hope that when the full horror of its consequences are seen we will shun it. God has made a world of cause and effect. This is as true of the spiritual and moral realm as it is of the physical world. Sow carrot seeds and you do not get cabbages. Sow selfishness and you do not reap a harvest of love. Those who sow the seeds of selfishness reap the bitter grain of loneliness.

St Paul explained it: 'Do not be deceived: God cannot be mocked. A person reaps what they sow' (Galatians 6). When we are brought face to face with the consequences of our actions we begin to see the true character of what we have done and who we are. The reaping of what we sow is an important way of knowing ourselves. It is not the case that we always learn from our mistakes. Yet it is in our failures that we have the opportunity to learn and to turn. If God always immediately delivered us from the disastrous consequences of many of our actions, so that we never had to live with what we had done, then we would be even less likely to obey his commandments. In seeing the results of our deeds we experience the judgement of God. It is a moment of truth. It is as if God is saying: 'This is the true nature of your action.' Such an experience of truth is designed by God to save us from following the path of self-destruction. That is why St Paul continued:

> The one who sows to please his sinful nature, from that nature will reap destruction; the one who sows to please the Spirit, from the Spirit will reap eternal life. Let us not become weary in doing good, for at the proper time we will reap a harvest if we do not give up. Therefore, as we have opportunity, let us do good to all people, especially to those who belong to the family of believers.
>
> (Galatians 6:8–10)

The other way in which God acts against evil is through the judgement of Jesus himself. As we enter into a relationship with Jesus through the pages of Scripture, through prayer and the sacraments we find that our lives are challenged by him. The way we treat people, our natures and ambitions, how we use our money, are slowly brought under the intense scrutiny of Jesus. He is the perfect model for the whole of humanity, the Son of Man. He stands for all that is good about being human. It is the work of the Holy Spirit today to impress him upon our minds and hearts. His goodness becomes the yardstick by which we measure and evaluate our actions and our being.

The Father has given Jesus authority to judge the world because he has, in flesh and in blood and with sweat and with tears, wrestled with the power of evil and the temptation to sin. We cannot say to Jesus: 'You know nothing of our struggles.' As we respond to the integrity of his life we inevitably find ourselves in the dust and crying with Peter, 'Lord, leave me for I am a sinful person'. His simple goodness both attracts and repels. We want him and dare to come close because of the beauty of his nature, yet at the same time we find that the purity of his character exposes the flaws in our own. God's judgement is at work. Through the presence of Jesus in the world God is shining his light to expose the sin and the evil.

Nicholas Wolterstorff[1] writes movingly about the face of God and asks why it is that the Bible says that no one could see the face of God and live. Perhaps we imagine that no one could behold his glory and splendour and continue to live. The author, who writes the book out of grief for his own son tragically killed in a climbing accident, imagines that if we could see the face of God what we would behold would be his sadness and his tears. Nobody could live if they were to see the pain in the eyes of God and his face lined with sorrow. This is the face of God that we see in Jesus Christ who with the love of God enters the world to act in judgement against evil and in mercy to rescue the oppressed.

This judgement and salvation of God is both a present and a

future activity. However much the modern Church may shy away from the Day of Judgement, it has always been a feature of orthodox Christian theology. It is a logical development of God's love and his passion for justice in his creation. If there were no day of reckoning, no redressing of the imbalance of good and evil, the poor and the oppressed, the victims of injustice, would rise up and question God's claim to be a God of justice.

It is the doctrine of universalism that all will be saved that has obscured the traditional belief in the Day of Judgement. The argument is that God's compassion will embrace the most reluctant and rebellious of sinners and that all in the end will be saved. It is clear from the life and teaching of Jesus that it is indeed God's desire that all should be saved. Yet in spite of all the love that Jesus showed the world, he clearly envisaged the possibility that some would wilfully place themselves beyond the experience of God's mercy. Mercy and forgiveness need to be received in order for them to be effective in restoring a relationship. This is as true in human relationships as it is in our relationship with God. If someone hurts you you can forgive them and promise to forget it; but if the other person will not receive the mercy then no matter how loving you are or for how long, the friendship remains broken. God in his love offers mercy and forgiveness as he weighs us in his scales of justice and finds us all wanting. If we resist his mercy we deny ourselves the healing benefits of his compassion.

Those who hold that on the last day all will surrender into the compelling love of God's embrace need to reflect that when people came face to face with the love of God in Jesus Christ many did yield but some hardened their hearts and set their face against him. Love did not conquer all. Love means giving people freedom. Freedom is a risk. Freedom means that people can choose. If on the Day of Judgement God then denies his beloved that freedom and compels them against their will to commune with him, then they are no longer the beloved but the coerced. If freedom is for this life only then it is only an illusion.

If God finally has his way with us regardless of our will it diminishes our worth and raises the question as to whether he genuinely loves us. The doctrine of judgement affirms God's love and his passion for justice; it sets the stage for the demonstration of his mercy.

3

The Authority of Jesus to Forgive

A few days later, when Jesus again entered Capernaum, the people heard that he had come home. So many gathered that there was no room left, not even outside the door, and he preached the word to them. Some men came, bringing to him a paralytic, carried by four of them. Since they could not get him to Jesus because of the crowd, they made an opening in the roof above Jesus and, after digging through it, lowered the mat the paralysed man was lying on. When Jesus saw their faith, he said to the paralytic, 'Son, your sins are forgiven.'

Now some teachers of the law were sitting there, thinking to themselves. 'Why does this fellow talk like that? He's blaspheming! Who can forgive sins but God alone?'

Immediately Jesus knew in his spirit that this was what they were thinking in their hearts, and he said to them, 'Why are you thinking these things? Which is easier: to say to the paralytic, "Your sins are forgiven," or to say, "Get up, take your mat and walk?" But that you may know that the Son of Man has authority on earth to forgive sins . . .' He said to the paralytic, 'I tell you, get up, take your mat and go home.' He got up, took his mat and walked out in full view of them all. This amazed everyone and they praised God, saying, 'We have never seen anything like this.'

(Mark 2:1–12)

People often speculate about the condition of this man and the possible causes of his paralysis. Commentaries on this passage by theologians begin to read like a doctor's medical notes! Was this illness physical or psychosomatic? Such enquiry is fruitless because we will never have access to the full facts of this man's medical history. Moreover, preoccupation with the cause of this man's illness is to overlook one of the most remarkable statements to be found on the lips of Jesus in any of the Gospels. 'Son, your sins are forgiven', is an assurance that is never found in the utterances of any other Jewish prophet. It is unique. Of course, the prophets were often the mouthpiece of God promising to forgive his people, such as the Lord saying through Isaiah: 'Come now, let us reason together though your sins are like scarlet they shall be as white as snow.' Yet nowhere else in Jewish literature do we find a prophet speaking so categorically and so absolutely, 'Your sins are forgiven'. Jesus' attention to this man's sins did not mean that he ignored his physical needs for as the story unfolds we see him caring for the whole person and healing him physically.

The first words that Jesus spoke to the paralysed man were, 'Your sins are forgiven'. This does not mean that his illness was caused by sin but rather that Jesus identified in him a universal need which is found in all people be they able-bodied, disabled or differently-abled. It may well have been that the friends who brought the man to Jesus and those standing around him believed that his illness had been caused by sin. Such a view was prevalent in the time of Jesus, as the episode of Jesus healing the blind man in John 9 showed: 'Who sinned, this man or his parents, that he was born blind?' It is a view that clouds the thinking of many people who suffer today. 'Why is God doing this to me? What have I done wrong? Why is God punishing me?' All these questions come from a heart tormented with the thought that my suffering is all my own fault, that I've brought this misery on myself through being so selfish and so offensive to God.

It may well be that such thoughts filled the head of the paralysed man. It would have been only natural. But we will never know. What we do know is that without any suggestion that sin was the cause, Jesus speaks initially to the person's primary need for forgiveness.

The question may well arise: if the cause of illness was not sin, why address that issue? The answer must be that Jesus deemed this to be a moment not only of pastoral care but also of divine disclosure.

This isn't a perfect picture! Some years ago I used to organize skiing holidays. Often in the party there would be at least one doctor. At the beginning of the holiday they would invariably ask me not to disclose the fact that they were doctors. They didn't want their holidays ruined by fellow skiers talking incessantly about their aches and strains on the slopes. One day one of the group fell badly just in front of an incognito doctor who, as he skied past, turned to see what had happened. Even behind his goggles I could see in his eyes the matter being weighed up. To stop and help would in an instant reveal to everybody just who he was. The moment of pastoral need would become a moment of revelation. And it did. He snow-ploughed to the side of the piste and made his way back up the slope. As he began attending to the injured skier his questions and his manner revealed all – his calling and his authority. Without having to say 'I am a doctor', everybody knew with relief that he was. He chose to make that moment of helping someone in need a moment of revelation. And from that point on his holiday became an endless round of informal consultations!

When Jesus was faced with the paralysed man he too had to weigh up the consequences of addressing the person's needs. To prescribe forgiveness for this dis-eased soul would further catapult him out of obscurity and disclose to the world the uniqueness of his character. To have kept silent about his authority to forgive would have denied the man what he most needed.

The recorded yet silent reaction of the religious leaders indicates exactly what Jesus was revealing in this moment of disclosure. 'Why does the fellow talk like that? He's blaspheming!

Who can forgive sins but God alone?' They were stunned. The roof had fallen in on them twice! To hear an itinerant preacher absolve someone unconditionally was scandalous to their ears. There was only one way to atone for sins and that was in the Temple, by offering sacrifices. This man had no authority to forgive anybody. Only God had the authority to lay aside some-one's sins: 'Who can forgive sins but God alone?'

What is remarkable is that this absolution from Jesus was uttered while the Temple was still standing and functioning. When Mark wrote his Gospel the Temple had not yet been destroyed. It was in the Temple that people found the oppor-tunity to atone for their sins and to hear that God would forgive his people. Yet no priest, no rabbi, no prophet would ever utter such an absolution, 'Your sins are forgiven'.

The point is often noted that Jesus nowhere says openly and explicitly, 'I am the Son of God'. But such a silence does not diminish his claim to divinity. Just as a doctor does not walk around his surgery proclaiming, 'I am a doctor' (indeed there would be something unnerving about such a person doing that!), but is revealed through what he does, so the authority and the divinity of Jesus are revealed by what he *does* in relation to other people. The announcement 'Your sins are forgiven' brings the bystanders into an awareness that they stand in the presence of an extra-ordinary man.

Whether it was the look on their faces or some supernatural insight or just a clever hunch, Jesus knew what was going on in their minds and challenged their presuppositions by asking a question: 'Which is easier; to say to the paralytic, "Your sins are forgiven" or to say, "Get up, take your mat and walk?" ' It's worth pondering how we might answer the question. In our culture the 'easier' thing to say would be 'Yours sins are for-given'. After all this is a statement that addresses the interior landscape of the personality. The truth or falsehood of the state-ment is not readily accessible to the eye of the outsider. You could say the words easily enough without anyone being able to contradict you. To say, 'Get up, take your mat and walk' is of a completely different order. It is a much harder thing to say because the truth or falsehood of the statement is soon established. If the man does not get up, pick up his mat and walk away then the claim is immediately invalidated and you have 'egg all over your face'. In our culture where words are cheap and miracles exceptional by far the easier thing to say would be 'Your sins are forgiven'.

But for Jesus the itinerant charismatic who had the power to heal the easier thing to say was 'Get up, take your mat and walk'. He had already experienced the surge of divine energy through his body as he touched Simon's mother-in-law and the man with leprosy. He had seen supernatural healing through his own hands. People with such powers were not uncommon in Jesus' day. But there was another dimension to saying 'Your sins are forgiven', which made it very much harder for Jesus to say it.

There was growing within him since childhood an awareness that his destiny lay in the hands of God his Father. He knew from early on that this destiny would set him at odds with those who were nearest him on earth. ('Didn't you know I had to be in my Father's house? But they did not understand what he was saying to them' Luke 2:49–50.) At the onset of his ministry he received affirmation from his Father when at his baptism God spoke from heaven: 'You are my Son, whom I love; with you I am well pleased' (Mark 1:11). God affirmed him as he entered the desert to wrestle with the dark forces of the evil one. Here he trod the frontiers of darkness and light, here he experienced the power of evil to defy God. It was in the desert that he saw the full scale of evil's empire. It was here that he realized what he was up against as the one charged by God – *in his very name* – to save and rescue God's people.

Exactly at what stage he knew that this destiny would involve him in sacrificing his own life we do not know. What we do know is that by the time he met the paralytic he knew he had extraordinarily the authority of God to absolve a stranger of his sins. It is not beyond the bounds of possibility that as well as knowing he possessed the divine authority to forgive he also knew the means by which that forgiveness would be assured. His own death. The sacrifice of his own life. If that is so then it was by far the hardest thing for him to say to the man 'Your sins are forgiven', for such an absolution was to involve him in the giving of his own life. 'Which is easier to say?' Certainly for Jesus it was not 'Your sins are forgiven'. That was the corridor of death-row, the scourging, the humiliation, the cross, the nails, the pain, the God-forsaken loneliness and death.

Having posed the question about which is easier, Jesus goes on to make the explicit and unequivocal statement that: 'The Son of Man has authority on earth to forgive sins.'

The phrase that is so often overlooked but which is pregnant with meaning is 'on earth'. It speaks of an experience of forgiveness here and now. In other words, we don't have to wait for heaven to be forgiven, we can be assured of forgiveness here on earth; we don't have to wait until we've done enough good deeds to cancel out the bad ones, we can be freed from our failure now. 'On earth' described the sphere of Jesus' authority as the Son of Man. He possessed the authority of God to declare the absolution of the sins of all those who walk the face of the earth. Here is the uniqueness of his ministry that makes him stand out amongst the crowd of prophets, rabbis, priests, teachers of righteousness and religious leaders.

Every religion offers men and women a means of coming to terms with their own frailty as human beings. In Islam the hope is extended that Allah, the merciful, will at a future moment have mercy on those who turn to him. The compassionate character of Allah accords with the Jewish and Christian understanding of God 'Who is slow to anger and rich in mercy'. But the claim of Jesus to have 'authority *on earth* to forgive sins' causes him to stand apart from Mohammed and other founders of the world's major religions. Anyone who comes to Jesus, submits to his authority and receives from him the absolution of his sins is in that moment forgiven and therefore liberated. The follower of Jesus doesn't just hope that one day God will forgive him but experiences in the moment of confession and absolution the assurance that his sins have already been forgiven. It is this very experience which led St Paul to say in the past tense, 'For it is by grace you have been saved' (Ephesians 2:10) and in the present tense 'Therefore there is now no condemnation for those who are in Christ Jesus' (Romans 8). St Paul, who had murdered Christians and persecuted Christ, came under the authority of Jesus and into the experience of forgiveness. This is what we celebrate in the Eucharist: 'The lamb of God who takes away the sins of the world.' This quote from St John doesn't say 'who will take away the sins of the world'. He announced with confidence that this is his present not future ministry.

I find that there are many people even in the Church today who are unaware of this authority of Jesus on earth to liberate them from their sins. Consequently, they live a life unnecessarily burdened with guilt and lacking the vitality that forgiveness brings. Their spiritual life is dulled.

Recently I was invited to preach at Choral Evensong in one of our great cathedrals. As a visiting preacher to a congregation of many visitors you have no idea who you are ministering to. The psalm set for the day was number 32:

Blessed is he whose transgression is forgiven,
whose sin is covered.
Blessed is the man to whom the Lord imputes no iniquity,
and in whose spirit there is no deceit.

I chose this as my text, ascended into the pulpit, the height of which made one feel even more distant from the congregation, and preached about the authority of Jesus on earth to forgive sins.

Within the week letters came from several people who had happened to be in the congregation that Sunday afternoon. One man wrote that he had been going to church all his life and had never until that service entered into the experience of being forgiven by Jesus, he had never before known the peace that flows from accepting the authority of Jesus to forgive you. Choral Evensong had come to him as a Damascus Road.

Knowing that Jesus has the authority now on earth to forgive us lies at the heart of Christian spirituality. This is our basic human need which God recognized at the incarnation.

The forgiveness of Jesus Christ has the power to reconcile us to God and to forge new relationships in the world. It is dynamic. It is also subversive. When a person comes under the authority of Jesus and is set free, his life and his values change. The old order of famous cliches such as 'looking after number one', 'give as good as you get', 'eye for an eye', and 'nobody does me down and gets away with it', give way to a new spirit of forgiving your enemies and praying for those who persecute you. This manifesto is more radical than any political agenda. Its source is to be found in a personal experience of the forgiveness of Jesus.

As Christians relate to people of other faiths they wonder about the significance of their own religion. Are all religions just the same? Are they simply different ways of viewing reality? It is in this saying of Jesus that the Son of Man has authority on earth to forgive sins that we find the distinctive feature of the Christian religion.

Recently I came across an unexpurgated version of *Robinson Crusoe*. Modern editions seem to leave out the description of how he finds his way to God. It is a moving passage in which he comes to experience Jesus Christ as his Saviour.

July 4th – In the morning I took the Bible; and beginning at the New Testament, I began seriously to read it, and imposed upon myself to read a while every morning and every night; not tying myself to the number of chapters, but as long as my thoughts should engage me. It was not long after I set seriously to this work, till I found my heart more deeply and sincerely affected with the wicked-ness of my past life. The impression of my dream revived; and the words, 'All these things have not brought thee to repentance', ran seriously in my thoughts. I was earnestly begging of God to give me repentance, when it happened providentially, the very day, that, reading the Scripture, I came to these words: 'He is exalted a Prince and a Saviour, to give repentance and to give remission.' I threw down the book; and with my heart as well as my hands lifted up to heaven, in a kind of ecstasy of joy, I cried out aloud, 'Jesus, thou Son of David! Jesus, thou exalted Prince and Saviour! give me repentance!' This was the first time I could say, in the true sense of the words, that I prayed in all my life; for now I prayed with a sense of my condition, and with a true Scripture view of hope, founded on the encouragement of the Word of God; and from this time, I may say, I began to have hope that God would hear me.

It is through the 'remission' of his 'wickedness' that Robinson Crusoe finds 'joy' and a freedom in prayer. This is the definitively Christian experience. Jesus exercises his authority over the earth and has the specific authority to forgive sins. Coming under that authority and seeking God's forgiveness through him brings us into an experience of freedom and peace.

Jesus Christ alone has the authority to take away the sins of all the world.

On BBC radio recently an expert on Japanese culture was being asked why Japanese soldiers were so cruel to their prisoners-of-war. The reason given was that to the Japanese mind surrender was an ignominious act that deserved only contempt. They despised those who surrendered and treated them accordingly. When the war ended with the surrender of Japan the people were faced with a great crisis for in surrendering they had made themselves contemptible. The Emperor of Japan, who at that time had the status of God among his people, declared that he personally took upon himself the shame, the ignominy and the guilt of his people's surrender. In so doing he set his people free.

In a more universal way Christ has taken to himself the sins not just of a nation but of the whole world. 'He himself bore our sins in his body on the tree, so that we might die to sin and live for righteousness; by his wounds you have been healed' (1 Peter 2:24). This taking into his wounded self of our sin liberates us and opens up the way to our healing.

As Jesus takes the sin to himself we see it cutting him off from his own Father as he cries out 'My God, my God why have you forsaken me'. In that moment sin comes to the heart of God himself as it lodges between God the Father and God the Son. As God the Creator (the Father, the Son and the Holy Spirit) is affected by this sin so all creation reverberates; the earth shakes, the rocks split, the graves burst open and darkness covers the earth (Matthew 27:51–52). In the orthodox liturgy for Good Friday, when this part of the Passion narrative is read, the people shake the chairs so that in the rattling they may remember the earthquake that provided the percussive accompaniment to the Saviour bearing the sins of the world.

The uniqueness of Jesus' death singles him out amongst the founders of the great world religions. No other leader dies to such effect. It is Jesus Christ's death as much as his life that endears him to his followers.

At a conference on inter-faith issues I heard a Hindu representative speak about the inclusiveness of Hinduism. He pointed out that in a Hindu shrine you would often see images of Krishna and Vishnu alongside those of Jesus and Mary. The attraction of Hinduism is that it is such a comprehensive faith embracing many diverse religious outlooks. The Hindu said that many people like him embraced Jesus and other Christian figures in their shrines.

During the conference I remarked that when a Christian embraces Jesus Christ he embraces also the forgiveness of God. I asked the Hindu whether Hindus have any such experience when they take Jesus into their shrines. 'There is no forgiveness in Hinduism', he replied. He went on to qualify this by saying that if a person showed forgiveness to someone who had wronged him then this would affect his Karma and influence the rewards or the punishments that he might receive in this life and in the next. Absolute forgiveness does present a problem to the Hindu for it undermines at a stroke the system of Karma.

While encouraging tolerance and respect for other faith communities, we would be lacking in both candour and integrity if we were to overlook the authority of Jesus to forgive people their sins. This authority is celebrated in our liturgies and expounded by every single book in the New Testament.

This authority to set people free from their sins is passed on by Jesus Christ to his disciples. 'If you forgive anyone his sins, they are forgiven; if you do not forgive them, they are not forgiven' (John 20:23). This aspect of the original disciples' ministry has been handed down and become part of the ministry of priests and presbyters. When priests (or presbyters) are ordained by the bishop he says to them: 'A priest is called by God . . . to call his hearers to repentance, and in Christ's name to absolve, and declare the forgiveness of sins (The *ASB* Ordinal).

Sometimes when people come to talk with me as their vicar they tell of burdens of guilt that they have secretly carried with them for years. It is often a great relief to pour out one's soul. But even though the sin has been confessed the sense of guilt remains. On one level, as a friend and counsellor you can encourage the person to seek God's forgiveness by confessing the sin to God and by promising to change his or her attitude and behaviour (repentance). The Bible contains the promise that: 'if we confess our sins God is faithful and just and will forgive us our sin and cleanse us from all unrighteousness' (1 John 1:9). Many people take God at his word and find forgiveness, remission of their guilt, freedom and peace. Some, however, need to hear that absolution articulated audibly by one of God's servants. Therefore, on another level, as a minister charged by God 'to absolve' I will ask such a person to say aloud to God what it is they are confessing and turning away from; I will then ask them 'the baptismal questions: Do you turn to Christ? Do you repent of your sins? Do you renounce evil?

After they have answered I will with the authority of Jesus
Christ absolve them:

> Almighty God
> who forgives all who truly repent,
> have mercy upon you,
> pardon and deliver you from all your sins
> through Jesus Christ our Lord. Amen.

Before I was ordained I counselled many people and where
appropriate encouraged them to *seek* God's forgiveness. Since
being a priest I have been able to *declare* God's forgiveness.
The dynamic is very different. Confidences prevent me giving
examples. But in many cases the difference is visible in the eyes
and on the face and in the person's posture and demeanour. It is
this dynamic liberation which is the essential experience of the
Christian for 'we have all sinned' (Romans 3) and 'if we say we
have not sinned the truth is not in us' (1 John 1). This experience
stems directly from the authority of Jesus on earth to forgive
sins.

I know someone who practised psychotherapy in California
very lucratively. One lady kept returning plagued with a heavy
sense of guilt. In the end the psychotherapist was moved to say
that what she needed was an experience of forgiveness. The lady
was indignant: 'I could go to church and get that advice and for
nothing.' The psychotherapist to his own surprise heard himself
saying: 'Well, perhaps you should.' (He's now a priest.) Psycho-
theraphy can be a valuable treatment especially when helping
those with neurotic experiences of guilt. But what no psychotherapist or any other therapist can offer is the absolution of
sins which is uniquely and authoritatively offered by Jesus
Christ.

4

The Authority of Jesus to Lay Down His Life

'I am the good shepherd. The good shepherd lays down his life for the sheep. The hired hand is not the shepherd who owns the sheep. So when he sees the wolf coming, he abandons the sheep and runs away. Then the wolf attacks the flock and scatters it. The man runs away because he is a hired hand and cares nothing for the sheep.

'I am the good shepherd; I know my sheep and my sheep know me – just as the Father knows me and I know the Father – and I lay down my life for the sheep. I have other sheep that are not of the sheep pen. I must bring them also. They too will listen to my voice, and there shall be one flock and one shepherd. The reason my Father loves me is that I lay down my life – only to take it up again. No one takes it from me, but I lay it down of my own accord. I have authority to lay it down and authority to take it up again. This command I received from my Father.'

(John 10:11–18)

It is widely acknowledged that in the time of Jesus shepherds were disreputable characters. ('An occupation which notoriously involved immorality and dishonesty and they were deprived of civil rights such as holding office or bearing witness on legal proceedings.'[1]) They had the same kudos in first-century Palestine as used-car salesmen have in our day! They had a notorious reputation for taking their master's sheep far away to find pasture, selling a couple *en route* and then, having pocketed the proceeds, returning home and saying, quite plausibly, that they had lost a few to wolves or thieves in the night. Along with tax-collectors and prostitutes they were seen as social outcasts and were often excommunicated from the local synagogue. This may be the reason why Jesus never says 'I am the shepherd'. He always qualifies the image by saying 'I am the good shepherd' as if it could not be taken for granted that a shepherd was always good.

The shepherd's dubious reputation makes it all the more remarkable that Luke should begin his Gospel with the account of the angels announcing the Good News of the birth of the Saviour to them. They were hardly the sort of group that an advertising executive would choose to endorse a product. It was tantamount to making the announcement to a convention of used-car salesmen! Why does Luke, who is so intent on commending the gospel, choose this story? It would hardly lend weight to his case. Many modern theologians question the historicity of the birth narratives. John McQuarrie, the eminent Oxford theologian, has written: 'The stories of apparitions of angels . . . however much they have come to be loved in Christian tradition, have no historical value and I suspect, very little theological value either.'[2]

The case for historicity is advanced by posing the question: What did Luke imagine he would gain by recording such an invention? Why does the gospel-writer undermine his own intention of proving 'the certainty' of the gospel events (Luke 1) by associating the story at the outset with such notoriously unreliable witnesses, people who were frequently disbarred from giving evidence in legal proceedings? Shepherds were not the sort of people you would call to a witness stand nor indeed were they an image you would choose to decorate the front of a seasonal greetings card! Modern theologians are in danger of having their thinking moulded by the latter-day impression of shepherds as romantic symbols of a rural idyll. They were no such thing in the Middle East in the first century. They were more like the Untouchables of Indian society. Outcasts, poorly paid, unreliable, despised and rejected.

In this description we begin to find the seeds of the theological reason for recording this unlikely event of the angels appearing to shepherds. Luke is famous for his portrayal of Jesus as a man of boundless compassion. Here is a man who shares his life with the poor, the outcasts, the despised and rejected. Theologically it is, therefore, entirely consistent for the angels to announce the Good News to such as them. From the beginning, the mission of Jesus is to rehabilitate those who are ostracized by the world. What modern theologians have overlooked is that on the hills of Bethlehem (Luke 2) God was already acting out the manifesto of Nazareth (Luke 4).

One day Jesus would pick up the baton from the angels who in the presence of the shepherds 'preach Good News to the poor . . . and to the oppressed proclaim the year of the Lord's favour'.

The scenario on the hills of Bethlehem has greater integrity within the story of the man from Nazareth, both theologically and historically, than much modern criticism allows. Jesus who associates with the poor and the powerless compares himself with the shepherd. He stands shoulder to shoulder with the outcast. 'I am the good shepherd.' At the same time he distances himself from the heartless and greedy practices that brought them into disrepute and emphasizes his qualities as 'the good shepherd'. These are that he knows his sheep by name, he keeps them safe, he provides them with pasture and life to the full.

One moment Jesus is describing himself as 'the good shepherd', the next he is talking of himself as 'the gate' (John 10:9). The clue to the mixing of these metaphors lies in the phrase that 'he lays down his life for the sheep'. Quite literally once the shepherd had gathered the sheep into the open pen he would lie across the entrance and guard them against thieves and wolves. Every sheep that entered that pen through that gate would be kept safe. 'I am the gate; whoever enters through me will be saved.' Jesus is both the good shepherd and the gate. In both images he is the one who lays down his life for the sheep.

This laying down of his life is both literal and symbolic, and is charged with meaning. It speaks of sacrifice and self-giving. In contemporary Christian doctrine and spirituality it is an idea that has gathered momentum so that 'self-giving' is the inspirational model of the incarnation that now motivates all Christian service. While I acknowledge the force of this aspect of the life and ministry of Jesus I want to fire some warning shots across the bow of this doctrinal ship and suggest that the overemphasis of the doctrine of self-giving borders on heresy, and its unqualified application to the life and ministry of a Christian is, at best, unbalanced and, at worst, destructive.

In many pastoral situations I have encountered people for whom the notion of total self-giving panders to their own particular psychological disposition. Take X for example: she's always helping other people, forever trying to solve their problems; she always seems on the edge of burning out; she acknowledges her own needs only in a very superficial way and allows no one to get near her, she always deflects any enquiry about her own health or well-being; she never allows anybody the opportunity of helping her, always insisting that others must be much worse off than she. Take Y for example: he sees everything in terms of tasks, as jobs to be done; he's energetic and plans his life and work strategically and efficiently; even though he looks ill he justifies his out-put in terms of preferring 'to burn out rather than rust away'; his prodigious ministry results in a family much neglected; those nearest and dearest are reminded either implicitly or explicitly that the man is doing the Lord's work and therefore find guilt added to their resentment that their father/husband has no time for them; whenever he's challenged about this life-style he shrugs it off, whenever anyone tries to reach him on an emotional level he parries the blow as if the potential friend were a boxer aiming for his solar plexus!

For both 'X' and 'Y' the doctrine of self-giving satisfies a neurosis. It is not the scope of these pages to analyse these

stereotypes psychologically and identify their needs. It is sufficient to note that there are many such people in the Church.
But the doctrine of self-giving must be challenged not primarily
for the sake of those people who misapply it and so justify
unwholesome lives but because it is wrong to isolate self-giving
and elevate it to the level of a virtue. It is wrong theologically. It
is wrong with reference to the example of Jesus. It is wrong since
Jesus never commanded his disciples to minister in such a way.

It is wrong theologically because such a doctrine does not
truly reflect the character of God. It has been pointed out by
theologians and by spiritual writers that God gives himself in
different ways. In creation, on the cross and in the renewing of
the Church, God the Father, Son and Holy Spirit are constantly
giving of themselves. This cannot be denied. Yet for us to draw
the conclusion that this was the great divine characteristic for all
to imitate would be exceedingly short-sighted.

To observe that the doctrine of the Trinity presents us with a
picture of God as persons-in-community each involved in giving
of themselves is surely only half the story. Each person gives to the
other. As the Gospel of John reveals, the Spirit glorifies the Son,
the Son glorifies the Father, the Father glorifies the Son. Each is
giving to the other. But if each is giving to the other then by
implication each is *receiving* from the other and each is glorified
by the other. Therefore, the Trinity is not a picture of mutual
self-giving but of mutual giving and receiving.

This is supported by the example of Jesus. Although he lays
down his life in an act of heroic self-giving there are many
instances when he received from others. He received ministry
from the Spirit at his baptism, encouragement from the angels
in the wilderness, affirmation from his Father at the Transfigur-
ation. He received hospitality from Mary and Martha and
friendship from Lazarus. Although he washed the feet of his
status-seeking disciples he let his own feet be washed with tears
and dried with the hair of a sympathetic woman. Here was a
model person who knew not only how to give but also how to
receive.

Giving and receiving is what makes a friendship. When the giving is all one-way and there is no receiving there can be no relationship of any depth. If a person only gives and refuses to receive how can you get close to him? It is in the mutuality of giving and receiving that relationships are forged and in which we realize the potential of our divine humanity. God is three-persons-in-community, giving and receiving of one another. To be fashioned in his image means that the human family is similarly a community of persons, giving and receiving. Whenever a person gives without receiving they not only impoverish their own lives but diminish the reflection of the divine image in human relationships.

This point emerges three chapters further on in the Gospel of John when Jesus washes the disciples' feet. I have explored some of the significance of this episode in *Servant*.[3] However, since writing it I have become aware of another dimension to the story. Not only does Jesus give us an example of self-giving servanthood by washing their feet but he challenges Peter's own reluctance to receive from Jesus. Thus this episode is as much about receiving as it is about giving. The point is eloquently made by Jesus when he says: 'You also should wash one another's feet. I have set you an example that you should do as I have done for you.' (John 13:14–15). This maxim is often interpreted as Jesus urging us to wash the feet of others. That is not what he says. He is not telling us here that we should go around disrobing ourselves and washing the feet and serving the needs of other people. What he says is much more radical, 'you should wash one another's feet'.

He is chiding and exhorting the disciples to look after *each other*. There's to be a mutuality about their service, a giving and receiving about their ministry. They are called to wash and be washed, to serve and be served. That is the example of Jesus. That is the example of the Trinity. If they can't receive as well as give then, as Jesus said to the reluctant and stubborn Peter, 'You have no part in me'. We can only have a part in and with Jesus when we receive as well as give. Our destiny to become like him, to become like God lies in being able to give of ourselves fully and to receive of others fully. That's the essence of community and of being fully human and of being divine.

It is no accident that in between the image of Jesus the Good Shepherd laying down his life for the sheep (John 10) and the episode of Jesus washing his disciples' feet (John 13), John records Mary in the home of her brother Lazarus pouring a pint of expensive perfume over the feet of Jesus. The house was filled with the fragrance of perfume (John 12). Here is Jesus receiving. There is no knowing what this gift did for Jesus. He was increasingly aware of his imminent death, an act of ultimate self-giving. He not only received the gift he also silenced the siren voices that doubted the value of spending so much money on Jesus. I do not think that it is an unspiritual or an exaggerated speculation to suppose that Jesus accepted the perfume and the caresses of Mary because he enjoyed and delighted in these affirmations.

To be able to receive is as much a part of being fully human and divine as is the ability to give. It was his character not only to give gifts but to receive them. The way Jesus accepted this ministry to himself provides us with a model, especially when we doubt the value of spending so much on ourselves. Whether it is finding time or energy or money for our own enjoyment there will always be a thousand and one other ways of spending the time, money or energy! What is more, there will always seem to be more important and worthier causes.

Yet very often other things are allowed to take priority because we do not have a God-given value of our own worth. We neglect ourselves and give of ourselves to others because we do not value ourselves enough. For all his self-giving Jesus had a proper sense of his worth: 'You will always have the poor, but you will not always have me.' Jesus was utterly committed to the poor but he was always aware of his own worth and his own needs. The giving of himself arose out of genuine love which is able to receive as well as give, rather than out of a self-loathing which can never receive from others. Yet there is a huge reluctance amongst many Christians to value themselves in this way. Such talk about receiving seems selfish and the antithesis of Christianity. But perhaps we need to challenge even the word 'selfish'. Breathing is selfish! It is an activity that promotes the well-being of the self. But it is not wrong. Caring for the self is a profoundly Christian ethic. To put it bluntly, if God loves us why should we hate ourselves?

So many expositions of Mary's anointing focus on the expense of the gift and the cost to the giver. That is right in so far as it is a comment on half the story. The fragrance of the perfume which filled the air also affirmed the worth of the recipient and his readiness to receive.

It is with this picture of Jesus as one who receives another's gift and so gives us an example of receiving gifts from others that we come to his self-giving for our sakes. The point should not be lost on us that it is only when we have learned from him how to receive that we ourselves shall be able to benefit from that which he gives. We are recipients before we are givers.

'I am the good shepherd . . . and I lay down my life for the sheep . . . The reason my Father loves me is that I lay down my life . . . I *lay it down* on my own accord. I have authority to *lay it down*' (John 10:14–18). This laying down of his life is emphatic. It is an icon of the shepherd who protects his sheep by lying across the entrance to the fold. The action of the shepherd ensures safety and life for the sheep. It is a high-risk action on the part of the shepherd since he is placing himself in the front-line of those who would attack the flock. Yet in spite of all the danger and indeed because of it the shepherd risks his own life by wilfully laying himself across the opening of the pen, thereby turning himself into a gate.

This icon is vivid and interprets the actions of Jesus as he lays down his life. He too ensures safety and life for his flock. Such a life-assuring sacrifice encourages one to choose the alternative translation 'I am the beautiful shepherd'. The beauty is found in the nobility and the courage of resolutely and emphatically laying down his life. He lays it down of his own accord; and he has authority to lay it down. Although Jesus fulfils the divine plan for the salvation of the world he is not some involuntary pawn on the chessboard of history who is moved against his will. The decision to offer himself for the salvation and the life of the world rests with him. And yet the decision was clearly premeditated.

Later on in the New Testament in the Book of Revelation John exchanges the picture of a shepherd with that of the lamb. Jesus is 'the Lamb that was slain from the creation of the world' (Revelation 13:8). This idea is reflected in 1 Peter where we read of the Lamb of God being 'chosen before the creation of the world' (1:20). The inference is that long before we were made and even before we had sinned God made provision for our forgiveness.

The arrival of Jesus on the stage is not some extemporary and *ad hoc* response to the needs of the world. His coming is premeditated. It is conceived in eternity. But the Lamb is an image of the passive victim, one whose life is taken away from him, against his will. In choosing the image of the Good Shepherd for himself Jesus is emphasizing his own authority in deciding to lay down his life. Much has been made by writers such as W. H. Vanstone[4] of Jesus, as he comes to the end of his life, moving from activity to passivity, from action to passion, from being the subject of the verb to becoming the object of the verb as he is handed over and the soldiers nail him to the cross. It is while Jesus is the object of the hurtful actions of others, while he is unable to do anything for himself, that on the cross he fulfils God's plan for the salvation of the world. In his example we find hope when we ourselves fall victim through illness, unemployment, disability. In a society which sets so much store by what people do and by implication undervalues those who are unable to do, the picture of Jesus as helpless victim on the cross yet fulfilling God's purpose is one of great hope. I would not wish to detract from the pastoral benefit of this important theological insight.

However the emphasis in the Fourth Gospel and particularly

in this picture of the Good Shepherd is that Jesus is in control of his destiny. He has the power to choose both what to do and when. Indeed it is his exercising of his freedom to lay down his life that continues to draw from his Father that love which always 'protects, trusts, hopes, perseveres'. The Good Shepherd cuts an independent figure. 'No one takes it from me, but I lay down of my own accord.' He was a person of destiny and power.

This notion fits uncomfortably with many contemporary presentations of Jesus. In order to show Jesus' solidarity with the poor and the disadvantaged he is projected as powerless. In terms of political power he was, of course, without any power-base. He stood outside the structures. But to emphasize his powerlessness – however noble a cause you wish to champion – is a nonsense. Jesus was a person of immense power. He could raise the dead, heal the sick, walk through crowds intent on killing him, feed the hungry, hold thousands spell-bound with his oratory, silence his critics and bring a nation to a standstill. Hardly the picture of a powerless man!

In the face of this evidence it is surprising that so many Christian commentators have inclined to make a virtue out of powerlessness. It is verging on the heretical. To be critical of the desire for power or the exercise of power, to be shy of celebrating power, to be reluctant to see Jesus as a person of power, to refuse to acknowledge the power that you yourself possess are familiar attitudes within the Church.

The very mention of the word in Christian circles has people flicking it away as if brushing dandruff off their shoulders. I was talking recently to someone who is in a position of immense power. He is a Christian. I drew attention to the fact that he possessed so much power. His instant reaction was negative. 'No, I don't like to think of it in terms of power.' 'Why not?' 'Power's something evil and manipulative.' Really?

It is clear that power has got itself a bad name through the abuses of it that haunt our history. But to deny power is to deny life itself. Life *is* power. A shoot bursts through the surface of the earth – there's power. Water cascades down a rock – there's power. The wind disturbs the trees – there's power. Fire destroys the coal and warms the hearth – there's power. A baby grips the finger of a parent – there's power. A person breathes – the ribcage expands and contracts – there's power. Life is power. What distinguishes the living from the dead is that the latter have no energy, no power, no life; they are lifeless and truly powerless. To make a virtue out of powerlessness is to make a virtue out of death.

What is all the more curious is that this emphasis on powerlessness has happened hand-in-hand with the discovery that the Christian faith is about liberating the oppressed. But there can be no liberation without the exercise of power. The process of setting people free is in itself an affirmation of the virtue of power. How and why power is used are critical questions. Obviously to use power to manipulate and diminish the worth of others is an abuse, whereas to use your power to set others free and enable them to realize their potential is good and right.

It is in this way that Jesus exercises power. He takes control of his destiny, wilfully spends his own life for the liberation and empowerment of others. Here is power. And it is good, a cause of celebration.

Paul Avis[5] draws a distinction between the New Testament words 'power' (*dunamis*) and 'authority' (*exousia*). Both words are used of Jesus. *Dunamis*/power is the strength, the might and the ability that belongs to the character of someone or something. It is used of Jesus when, for example, the woman touches him in the crowd and he senses that *dunamis*/power has gone out of him. *Exousia*/authority is not just the ability to perform an action but the right and the freedom to do so which has been conferred by a higher authority. '*Exousia* is the right that lies behind the exercise of power (*dunamis*), though the two terms are sometimes used almost synonymously.' It is the word *exousia*/authority that provides the thread that sows together the chapters of this book. The authority that Jesus possessed is that which comes from the Father. It is something that is divinely given from within the Godhead (see Matthew 28:18). It is with this divine authority that he exercises power to liberate the oppressed. Not only does he possess the authority to judge he also possesses the authority to forgive; not only does he possess the authority to drive out evil he also possesses the authority to heal; not only does he possess the authority to lay down his life he also possesses the authority to take it up. With this authority he exercises power to set free those whose lives are dogged by evil, failure, disease and death. It is because he comes with authority and the power to liberate that his message is one of Good News.

The authority of Jesus shone through his personality, through his bearing, his actions and what he said. Avis quotes Shakespeare's Lear:

Lear: What wouldest thou?
Kent: Service.
Lear: Whom wouldest thou serve?
Kent: You.
Lear: Dost thou know me fellow?
Kent: No, sir; but you have that in your countenance which
      I would fain call master.
Lear: What's that?
Kent: Authority.

5

The Authority of Jesus to Take Up His Life

> *'The reason my Father loves me is that I lay down my life –
> only to take it up again. No one takes it from me, but I lay it
> down of my own accord. I have authority to lay it down and
> authority to take it up again. This command I received from
> my Father.'*
>
> *At these words the Jews were again divided. Many of them
> said, 'He is demon-possessed and raving mad. Why listen to
> him?'*
>
> *But others said, 'These are not the sayings of a man pos-
> sessed by a demon. Can a demon open the eyes of the blind?'*
>
> *(John 10:17–21)*

In John 10 the word 'life' has two meanings and in the original
Greek two separate words are used. *Zoe* is the life that emanates from God. It is the life that Jesus has authority to give: 'I
have come that they may have life, and have it to the full' (John
10:10). 'For you granted him authority over all people that he
might give eternal life to all those you have given him' (John
17:2). The life of God that Jesus has authority to give is 'full' and
'eternal'. We shall explore this in Chapter 8. This life is different
from what Jesus is referring to here when he says: 'I have
authority to lay down my life and to take it up again.' The word
here is *psuche* which means not only the heart and mind of an
individual but also his very personality. In contrast to *zoe* which
is the life of God breathed into an individual, *psuche* is the
individual living being himself. It is this living being, this life, this

personality that is on the line when we deny ourselves, take up a cross and follow Jesus. 'Whoever shall lose his *psuche*/life for my sake and for the gospel will save it' (Mark 8:35). And it is this *psuche*/life that Jesus lays down when he himself is crucified and it is this very *psuche*/life which, after his death, he has the authority to take up again. In this passage John has Jesus anticipating his resurrection from the dead, his taking up of that which he has laid down in sacrifice.

On the grounds of this text alone the nature of that resurrection is unclear. It is possible to argue that what is imagined is continuation of the personality of Jesus beyond death. It is at least that. But is it more than that?

The Gospel which records the most resurrection appearances is Luke. It is agreed by scholars that the evangelist was writing an apologia, a defence of the Christian faith to a non-Jewish culture. The world was dominated by the military and economic power of the Romans and by the philosophical ideas and language of the Greeks. That is why the New Testament is written in a form of Greek. Luke's aim and that of the Christian community which propagated his account was to demonstrate the integrity of the Christian faith and its acceptability to those beyond the Jewish community:

> Christian preachers and apologists learned to use the thought forms and the language of Hellenistic philosophy and religion. In a word, they learned to present their faith in such wise that it cohered with, as it modified, the contemporary religions and scientific world picture.[1]

The use of the Greek language to write their accounts was the first step in this direction.

At the risk of over-simplification the view which held sway in the Graeco-Roman world was that the body was a prison to the soul. Death was an experience to be embraced because with the mortification of the flesh the soul was liberated to return to God. It was thought that matter was inherently evil and that the soul, which was good, immortal and imprisoned in the flesh, could on death continue on its journey and be united with God. There was no place in this scheme of things for the continuation of the body beyond death. The idea was anathema. That is not to say that they welcomed death. It harboured the same fears as it does for us all. But for the high-minded like Plato and Socrates, who articulated the philosophy of the age, death was not an evil but a good. 'No one knows whether death, which men in their fear apprehend to be the greatest evil, may not be the greatest good.'[2] According to Plato the body, because it contained the seeds of its own destruction, was inherently evil: 'The body's particular flaw is disease, which weakens and destroys it, till finally it ceases to be a body at all ... the result is annihilation.'[3] He saw the immortal soul as longing to associate with 'the divine and immortal and eternal' and of being quite 'unaffected by fever or disease or injury or even by the body being cut to fragments'. The physical realm of the body and the material world ranked lower than the realm of the soul.

Given that this was the prevailing view in the Graeco-Roman world it is both surprising and significant that the one evangelist committed to engaging with the culture records in such detail the physical dimensions of the bodily resurrection of Jesus. Had he written that the soul of Jesus had been liberated by the death of his body and that this immortal soul was now embarked upon the journey of being united with 'the divine/immortal and eternal' it would have found ready acceptance among the Greeks and the Romans. This was their understanding of the nature of things. But the fact is that Luke, the evangelist and apologist, does no such thing. On the contrary, he records five resurrection appearances of Jesus which present him as audible, visible and tangible after his death. They are not individual subjective experiences because the sightings are experienced by more than one person. It is Paul who, in a document dated earlier than Luke's Gospel, records that one of those resurrection appearances was to over five hundred people at one time (1 Corinthians 15). The telling phrase is his throwaway line 'most of whom are still living' (1 Corinthians 15:6). In other words we are not in the period of myths and legends which gather momentum and accretions only after the original eye-witnesses have died and can no longer be called on to testify.

Even the most superficial reading of the Letters to Corinth show that at the heart of the Graeco-Roman world Paul had to contend with the sceptics who, long before the Age of Reason and the Enlightenment, questioned the resurrection of Jesus. What were they questioning? It was not the view that the soul of Jesus continued after death that they were challenging and found difficult to believe. This was their own belief. There was nothing in this for the Greeks to challenge! The body is dead; long live the immortal soul: this was their creed. Thus, when Paul rises to the challenge 'if Christ has not been raised' six times in Chapter 15, what he is defending is not the continuation of the soul of Jesus but his bodily resurrection from the dead, and yes, the empty tomb. Either the tomb is empty or, as he says, 'our faith is empty', as hollow as the shell of an Easter egg. The reason why the Greeks in Corinth found the resurrection of Jesus so hard to believe was because it was a *bodily* resurrection and it was inconceivable to them that their salvation lay in the story of one whose body continued beyond the grave. The body was about decay, destruction and evil; for the Greeks it was the soul that was good and immortal.

The question persists: Why did the third evangelist insist on bringing his account of the life and death of Jesus to a climax by recording the bodily dimensions of the resurrection? What purpose would it serve? How could he square such an obstacle to faith with his desire to persuade his audience? It ran counter to the culture. It was an obstacle to them embracing the message of Jesus Christ. In my own reasoned and devotional reading of the New Testament I have come to the conclusion that Luke records these unforgettable, disturbing and incredible events because these are the things which actually happened.

Thus Luke gives an example to all Christians who are sent to engage with their culture. We must use every means to render the message as accessible as possible in the language and the ideas. But, in the end, the culture must always be challenged wherever its ideas and values run counter to what God has revealed. The Graeco-Roman world's view about the body, the soul and death ran counter to what God had demonstrated in the life, death and bodily resurrection of Jesus Christ. Truth must out. It had to be told even under pain of death. And it was.

This is not to deny that there are difficulties in the text when it comes to holding together the different accounts of the resurrection. John Weham[4] has attempted a correlation. What this affirms is that when Luke wrote his Gospel and when a Jew like Paul preached the resurrection of Jesus from the dead, it was a stumbling block to the Greeks to accept a bodily resurrection. In the current debates about the resurrection it comes across that it is only in this age of science that we have a problem and, by implication, that in New Testament times it was all perfectly acceptable. Such a view ignores the cultural context which Luke and Paul were bearing witness in and contending with.

The bodily resurrection of Jesus has significance theologically. The division of the person into three categories of mind, body and spirit was foreign to the Jewish understanding of humanity. A person was an integrated whole. To those Jews who believed in the resurrection of the dead (the Sadducees did not, the Pharisees did) there was no such thing as a resurrection which did not involve the body. In Daniel 12 we hear: 'multitudes who sleep in the dust of the earth will awake; some to everlasting life, others to shame and everlasting contempt'. Although the passage is full of imagery there is continuity between the persons 'asleep in the dust' and 'awake', and no reference to disembodied spirits. Yet the theological significance of the bodily resurrection is that the material as well as the spiritual comes within the eternal purposes of God. As John Polkinghorne has said: 'The bodily resurrection of Jesus Christ demonstrates that matter matters to God.'[5]

The resurrection of the body of Jesus has profound social implications. If it was only the soul of Jesus that had lived on we could conclude that the most important aspect of the Church's mission is to convert and care for the soul, and that the material needs of people are of only secondary importance. But the bodily resurrection shows that God values the body as well as the soul and that his eternal plan encompasses the material as well as the spiritual. The bodily resurrection of Jesus Christ traces its origins back to the opening chapter of Genesis where God deems the whole of his material creation 'good'. This double affirmation of the material by God is the context in which Christians are called to minister to the social as well as the spiritual needs of the world. God calls us to care for every aspect of his creation because he himself is committed to it. To be committed to the Risen Lord Jesus means to be committed to his creation, material and spiritual, because 'all things were created by him and for him' (Colossians 1:16).

There is an inextricable link between the bodily resurrection of Jesus and the cause of social justice. If it is the soul only that has an eternal destiny then feeding the hungry, freeing the oppressed, fighting injustice are poor and distant cousins to the task of saving souls. But the resurrection of the body challenges such a heresy. It proclaims that to care for the whole person is a reflection of God's commitment to his creation in all its dimensions.

The subordination of the body to the soul has been responsible for the way many Christians have retreated from politics, social action, the arts, sexuality and other aspects of the material world. The root of the problem lay with the hellenization of the gospel whereby the Greeks overturned the healthy and earthy attitudes of the Jews by insisting that the body was inferior to the soul. That is why Paul's preaching about the resurrection to the Corinthians and Luke's insistence on the bodily resurrection to Theophilus are such crucial testimonies. They challenged the world-view which valued the soul and in the same breath denigrated the body.

The gospel founded in the death and bodily resurrection of Jesus signals a godly and healthy regard for the body. It opens up the way to valuing the material and to seeing that feeding the poor, freeing the oppressed and fighting injustice are of primary importance. They are expressions of God's commitment to the material world which he again deemed 'good' by raising the material and physical body of his Son Jesus Christ from the grave.

In conclusion, here is a curious observation. That part of the Church which has been vociferous about the social implications of the gospel has been the most diffident about affirming the bodily resurrection, and that other part of the Church which has been quick to proclaim the supernatural dimension of the empty tomb has been slow to match this preaching of personal salvation with a theology of social action. The tragedy of this division is that it has contributed, more than many realize, to the relegation of Christianity to the level of purely spiritual and private experience. A rediscovery of the theological significance of the bodily resurrection will give the Church confidence to know that the gospel speaks to the whole of God's creation: to the material as well as the spiritual, to the social as well as the personal, to the public arena as well as the private domain. Whether the world at large will listen is another matter. But such a theological awaking would renew the Church for its mission to serve the whole of God's world which he loves and for whom he sent his Son.

6

The Authority of Jesus Over Evil

Jesus withdrew with his disciples to the lake, and a large crowd from Galilee followed. When they heard all he was doing, many people came to him from Judea, Jerusalem, Idumea, and the regions across the Jordan and around Tyre and Sidon. Because of the crowd he told his disciples to have a small boat ready for him, to keep the people from crowding him. For he had healed many, so that those with diseases were pushing forward to touch him. Whenever the evil spirits saw him, they fell down before him and cried out, 'You are the Son of God.' But he gave them strict orders not to tell who he was.

Jesus went up into the hills and called to him those he wanted, and they came to him. He appointed twelve – designating them apostles – that they might be with him and that he might send them out to preach and to have authority to drive out demons.

(Mark 3:7–15)

The many gospel stories of Jesus driving out demons display his authority over evil. The way he acts against the evil spirits is consonant with his authority to judge. In driving out the demons he is pushing back the frontiers of evil and reclaiming the earth for the rule of God. Like a bulldozer driving into and destroying the barricades, Jesus challenges the sway of evil over the earth; he confronts darkness with light. As with his authority to judge, the authority of Jesus over evil spirits is consistent with the love of God. As surely as love is committed to excising whatever is destroying the beloved, so love is bound also to exorcize whatever is desecrating that which love cherishes.

Modern scholarship has led us to be sceptical about these stories of demon-possession, preferring to understand them in terms of mental illness or epilepsy. The description of the symptoms do appear identical to other conditions which today we would urgently say have nothing at all to do with demonic influence. It is appalling to think that someone who suffers from epilepsy or schizophrenia should be deemed demon-possessed.

My own pastoral experience however has led me to believe that although we must always seek medical counsel for bizarre and irrational behaviour, we must not close our minds to the possibility of an external evil influence in the lives of some people. Although I have to admit that the prevailing intellectual climate is against such a view.

In our culture there is a widespread denial of moral absolutes. If there is no absolute Truth, no absolute Right then it follows that there is no evil in any absolute sense. (It has always struck me as curious that to affirm that there is no absolute Truth is a contradiction in terms since, at the very least, you are holding this opinion to be absolutely true!) Everything is relative to personality, conditioning and culture. However attractive and prevailing this outlook is, it has the most appalling implications. It means that the oppression of blacks by whites, the brutalizing of children in refugee camps, the massacre of millions of Jews, the rape of women are only *relatively* wrong. The perpetrators have simply been conditioned to do such things, they are products of their social environment. The fact that decent and civilized people deem them and their behaviour to be wrong means only that they have been differently conditioned, products of a different social environment. But when Christians say that oppression is wrong and ought to be stopped we are doing more than expressing a cultural opinion, we are speaking as if there were some moral absolute binding on all people, regardless of their culture, which is being violated. Admittedly those absolutes are not always crystal clear and they have to be worked out in different and specific contexts but nevertheless there is a source and an authority to our moral perceptions that is beyond our own personality and culture. This is God. But when God is dethroned the absolutes dissolve like sugar in hot water; there is neither Good nor Evil in any absolute sense.

It is against such a background that contemporary biblical scholarship has wrestled with the meaning of these stories about Jesus exorcizing evil. By and large the notion of a supernatural and evil personality resisting God and influencing the world has been either rejected or ignored. Furthermore, the insights of modern psychiatry have tended to dismiss patients' confessions of demon-possession as a type of religious mania. In many instances this has, as I have witnessed, been a correct diagnosis. But to deny the reality of an external evil influence in the world altogether is to contradict Jesus' perception of the kingdom of God and the pastoral and evangelistic experience of many people in the Church today across the world.

These chapters are being penned in the aftermath of the James Bulger murder and of other horrific stories of children abused and murdered. News programmes have been saturated by expert opinions as to why, in a period of our history when there has never been so much health-care, education and social security, there should be such brutality. People have pointed to the high incidence of divorce, unemployment and alienation. Experts have high-lighted many social and psychological factors. These all afford important insights but have still left people perplexed as to the provenance of such barbaric cruelty. What we are witnessing is more than human frailty or even selfishness. There is a spiritual dimension to our existence that can be influenced by external forces of good or evil. According to the experience and teaching of Jesus there is a spiritual power of evil, that is pledged to plunge the world into darkness so that where there is love, hatred will supplant it; where there is pardon, the thirst for revenge will overtake it; where there is faith in God, selfishness will suffocate it; and where there is hope, it will be drowned in despair. This is the spiritual chaos that the evil one seeks every opportunity to conspire to create. This is not to describe a primitive culture; it is today's world, evidenced in the sado-masochistic video-nasties, the killing of children, the pornographic exploitation of women, the exploitation of the poor, the clouded judgement that makes the powerful impervious in their imagination to the barely audible crying of the weak. The evil one triumphs in the darkness, where there is no light, for in the darkness people cannot see nor can they then feel the plight of those they maim, manipulate and destroy. The last thing that the demons of darkness want is light: 'Everyone who does evil hates the light, and will not come into the light for fear that his deeds will be exposed' (John 3:20).

There is a spiritual source to the malaise in the world. To deny this is to overlook the insights of orthodox Christian doctrine; to ignore it is to make the wrong diagnosis and to write the wrong prescription both socially and pastorally.

Even as I write I hear the objection that belief in demons belongs to the mind-set of the Middle Ages rather than to the enlightened understanding of the twentieth century. Certainly we can abandon the pictures of impish figures in black with horns and tails and ghoulish faces. But it is not fanciful to believe that there is an unseen spiritual dimension to reality; that this realm is peopled by spiritual beings who within the sovereignty of God exercise, like us, a freedom to choose between good and evil; that, like us, their choices and their actions affect the lives of others. It is clear that Jesus saw the world in those terms and that integral to his understanding of his mission and of the kingdom of God was the idea of rescuing people not only from the internal power of sin but from the external influences of evil. Although Jesus was a child of his time and his thinking was shaped by his culture, most would agree that his experience and understanding and knowledge of God was more intimate than that of any other prophet. His perception of the divine, of the eternal and of reality was that the struggle between good and evil, which we witness daily on our TV screens, is a conflict that rages not just in the physical world but in the spiritual realm also.

I find it interesting through contact with young people in schools, that they are more aware of the reality of a supernatural force of evil than they are of God. Many will have taken part in a Ouija board session or seance and tried to make contact with the supernatural realm. For many these will have been fascinating yet disturbing experiences. Whereas they will offer up all sorts of scientific and rational objections to a belief in God, they often have experience of contact with the spirit world which has left them frightened and wary.

Recently two men were installing some equipment in my office in the church. Out of the blue one of them asked outright, 'Do you believe in evil?' Before venturing an answer I asked him if he did. He proceeded to tell a story of how his fiancée had been put under a curse by her family, how her personality had changed and how the house they had bought was now visited by strange supernatural happenings. We talked for a long time together. When I offered to pray with them the two men instinctively knelt on the floor. As I prayed I focused on Jesus, the light of the world, who alone has the power to dispel the darkness. What struck me through this providential meeting was the certainty of the man's experience and awareness of evil, and the readiness with which he accepted the invitation to pray to Jesus. I am convinced that the gospel episodes of Jesus encountering the forces of darkness speak to us of more than a dark side to human nature: they reveal a hidden world of evil that is real and external and which manifests itself both in social structures and even in individual personalities who deliberately open themselves up to the evil one and his angels.

The enemy of darkness is light. When Jesus, the light, appeared on the world's stage, right from the first act there were plots to extinguish the light. From Herod's child-abusing and murderous strategies to the demonically inspired treachery of Judas (John 13), the antagonism of darkness to light was evident. This encounter in Mark's Gospel, which Vincent Taylor in

his Greek Commentary is convinced reflects 'primitive testimony', shows a typical conflict between Jesus and the unclean
spirits of the evil one.

Graham Twelvetree[1] has written a detailed exposition of
Jesus' encounters with demonic activity in the Gospels. Here in
this chapter I confine myself to pointing up certain aspects of
this episode in Mark 3 which are of significance.

The scene Mark paints so vividly verges on chaos. The people
are crowding forward to touch Jesus as he takes the practical
step of ordering his disciples to get ready a small boat. In the
midst of the tumult the evil spirits scream out 'You are the Son
of God'. For various reasons the Gospels present us with Jesus'
reluctance to identify himself and here he responds by ordering
the spirits to be silent. But what were the spirits doing by exposing the identity of Jesus? In the more developed Gospel of John
we learn that it is the work of the Holy Spirit to reveal the truth
about Jesus. But here that work is being done, usurped, by the
unclean spirits. Why? The details of Mark's account show Jesus
in a vulnerable situation with 'a large crowd', 'many people',
'crowding him' and 'pushing forward to touch him'. Jesus'
decision to get into the boat was clearly for self-protection. It is
not inconceivable that the aim of the evil spirits in declaring the
identity of Jesus was to add to the mayhem of the crowd and to
crush the life out of Jesus. The strategy of the evil one is to find
our weaknesses and to exploit them. The realm of darkness was
being threatened by the advent of the light; people were being
healed and rescued from the snare of evil; the instinctive reaction of the angels of darkness was to do all in their power to
snuff out the light. To that end, they were even prepared to do
what hitherto only the angels of light delighted in doing, namely
announcing the arrival of the Son of God. There was method in
their madness. The strategy of the evil one is not the firing of
indiscriminate volleys. It is a methodical playing to our weakness. When St Paul urged the Christians at Ephesus to withstand
the evil one by cladding themselves with the armour of God, he
warned them to stand against 'the wiles' of the Devil. The

Greek word he uses is 'methods'. There is method in his madness.

I know that there are many excesses, especially in some of the extreme wings of the Church. I have witnessed these excesses first-hand and can understand why many Christians dismiss demonology altogether. I know too that emphasis on the power of spirits can be used by some people to exonerate themselves of responsibility for their own lives and actions. But I also believe that the modern Church is failing in its ministry to the world if it fails to recognize the power of the demonic in human affairs, both corporately and personally. It was Baudelaire, the French poet, who put the words into the mouth of one of his characters, saying that the Devil's greatest trick was to persuade us that he doesn't exist. Often when I pray the Lord's Prayer and come to the petition 'deliver us from evil', I change it to 'deliver us from the evil one' (which is a legitimate alternative translation of the Greek). It reminds me that the struggle is not just with my flawed nature but with external influences that conspire against peace, goodness and God. As St Paul wrote: 'For our struggle is not against flesh and blood, but against the rulers, against the authorities, against the powers of this dark world and against the spiritual forces of evil in the heavenly realms' (Ephesians 6:12). This awareness of the physical and spiritual dimensions of evil permeates the whole of the New Testament. Any spirituality that lays claim to being biblical ought to reflect that consciousness. Recently I was speaking at a conference on this very subject and learned that an African version of the Lord's Prayer keeps this truth before the petitioner: *Utuokoe na yule Mwovu* (May you save us from that evil one).

It is interesting that St Paul uses the word *exousia* for the authorities that exercise an evil influence over the world. On the one hand we have the authority of Jesus, on the other we have the authority of the evil one. Using the same word for both could lead us to the conclusion that good and evil were evenly matched in their struggle. This is a view that is commonly held by those who concede that there is a spiritual dimension to reality. They believe the world is finely balanced between the forces of light and darkness. But a reading of the Gospels and the rest of the New Testament leads one to reject such a dualistic understanding of the Universe. The Christian recognizes the extent of the power of the evil one but knows that the sovereign power of God is greater; he knows that when darkness meets light darkness is always defeated; he knows that the authority of Jesus is greater than the authority of the evil one. Mark is the first Gospel writer to recognize this. When Jesus was challenged and threatened by the 'evil and unclean spirits' he gave them strict orders not to tell who he was (3:12). Throughout his account of the ministry of Jesus, Mark shows him as one who exercises authority over the evil spirits who even though they would destroy him are compelled to obey him. It is pastorally, as well as theologically, important, when making people aware of the reality of evil to point up the truth that Jesus Christ is *Lord*. We do not live in a dualistic universe where good and evil are evenly balanced. The devil is no match for Jesus however much he may continue to try to destabilize the world. His days are numbered.

One of the words for the evil one found in the Gospels is *Beelzeboul* (Mark 3:22) 'the Prince of demons'. The origin of the word is unclear. It could mean 'Lord of the High Places' or 'Lord of the Air', the former referring to the altars of sacrifice known as 'High Places', the latter referring to the air, the realm of the invisible spirits. In the early periods of the Old Testament *Ba'al* meaning Lord or Master was used of Yahweh but by the time of Hosea it was rejected as a title for God: 'In that day' declares Yahweh 'you will no longer call me Ba'al' (Hosea 2:17). Indeed, by the time of Elijah, *Ba'al* was the word that described any spiritual power that challenged the authority of Yahweh.

The name *Beelze*boul was often corrupted into *Beelze*bub which means 'Lord of the Flies'. It first appears in the Bible as a title for the god of Ekron (2 Kings 1). 'Beelzebub' was a way of belittling the authority and power of another deity. It was a derisive title. This god is no more than a god of flies! It revealed a healthy outlook. The Prince of demons may well be active in this world undermining the authority of God and enslaving people in darkness but when it comes to a straight contest between him and the God of Jesus Christ he is no match. This understanding of the authority of Jesus over the minions of the evil one is pastorally important because in some of the excessive focusing on demonic activity you could be forgiven for thinking that it was Jesus who was Lord of the flies. To know that Jesus Christ is Lord of heaven and earth is to affirm that he is Lord over all creatures, physical and spiritual.

At our baptism as well as being asked 'Do you turn to Christ?' and 'Do you repent of your sins?', we are also asked 'Do you renounce evil?'. This question deliberately challenges us to disengage from every influence of the evil one. In declaring 'I turn to Christ' and 'I renounce evil' we are stating publicly our conscious change of allegiance. By placing ourselves under the authority of Jesus we are confessing publicly that God has 'rescued us from the dominion of darkness and brought us into the kingdom of the Son he loves, in whom we have redemption, the forgiveness of our sins' (Colossians 1:13–14). Christian mission is about rescuing the whole world, its structures, communities and individuals, from the dominion of darkness; it is about bringing the whole world under the authoritative lordship of Jesus Christ. We know that while there is still time, the evil one will attempt to thwart and destabilize the world and the Church. But the authority that Jesus possessed he gives to his disciples.

The seventy-two returned with joy, and said, 'Lord, even the demons submit to us in your name.'

He replied, 'I saw Satan fall like lightning from heaven. I have given you authority to trample on snakes and scorpions, and to overcome all the power of the enemy; nothing will harm you. However, do not rejoice that the spirits submit to you, but rejoice that your names are written in heaven.'

(Luke 10:17–20)

Having authority over evil means actively challenging institutions and structures that enslave people in darkness as well as ministering to people personally in prayer and counselling. But Jesus warns us against triumphalism. Here is servant authority. There is no joy to be found in the defeat of the enemy, not even in Satan's tragic and inevitable end; the joy is to be found in the new heaven and the new earth which, free from evil, will be the dwelling place of God with his people where: 'There will be no more death or mourning or crying or pain, for the old order of things has passed away' (Revelation 21:4).

7

The Authority of Jesus to Heal

*He called his twelve disciples to him and gave them authority
to drive out evil spirits and to cure every kind of disease and
sickness.*

*These are the names of the twelve apostles: first, Simon
(who is called Peter) and his brother Andrew; James son of
Zebedee, and his brother John; Philip and Bartholomew;
Thomas and Matthew the tax collector; James son of
Alphaeus, and Thaddaeus; Simon the Zealot and Judas
Iscariot, who betrayed him.*

(Matthew 10:1–2)

As well as giving his followers the authority to drive out evil
spirits, Jesus gives them the authority to heal every disease and
sickness. For various reasons there has been a renewed emphasis upon the miracles of Jesus and the healing ministry of the
Church. This had been overlooked until recently because
modern scholarship had played down the reliability of these
stories in the Gospels. And, although those reservations remain
with some scholars, the culture of Western civilization, which
engulfs the Church in the West, has so changed and become so
obsessed with healing and health that the Church has responded
with its rediscovery of Jesus' healing ministry. My own view is
that it is extremely unlikely that a Christology of Jesus would
ever have emerged which proclaimed him as a life-giving and
peace-endowing figure if there had been no foundation in fact
that he brought healing to people's dis-eased lives. As Edward

Schillebeeckx has written: 'Christology without a historical foundation is empty and impossible.'[1]

In the time of Jesus the diseased, the lepers and the disabled *were* the poor. As far as they were concerned there was only one form of good news for the poor; to be made better. Anybody who came with lofty sentiments about God caring for the poor and who did not do something about it practically would, to use St Paul's vivid image, be as irritating as 'a clanging symbol'. Good news for the poor and the sick had to be more than words, word, words.

Could Jesus have started workshops for the disabled, hospices for the dying, work programmes for the unemployed, hospitals for the sick, could he have challenged the economic and political oppression of the Roman authorities? All this would have showed the poor and the sick that God was as concerned with their physical needs as he was with their souls. After all, God had made them, body and soul, and anyone claiming for his mission a mandate from God would be expected to show his love practically and in material ways. But such programmes would have been a lifetime's work. Indeed, it has taken many societies umpteen generations to develop these sorts of programmes, many of them directly inspired by the example of Jesus in caring for both the soul and the body.

How was Jesus to show the poor (and the rich) that the rule of God was about to impact the world in a new and more radical way?

How was Jesus to tell the sick and the poor the Good News that God loved them? He healed them. The healing was spiritual and physical. Through these miracles they were made well and, able-bodied, could work again and care for themselves and their families. They found their dignity. This is not to say that there is no dignity for the disabled. It is simply recognizing that in the time of Jesus sickness was a direct cause of poverty, especially where those illnesses such as leprosy caused you to be excommunicated from society. Good news for the sick, the outsider, the poor meant being healed. It was through his very acts of physical healing that Jesus gained a reputation for being the messenger of Good News for the *poor*. It is inconceivable that anyone would have believed his claim to be the herald of Good News for the poor if he had not healed the sick, the outcast and the poor. Without the healing of the poor his words would have been empty. Wherever Jesus healed the sick 'Jesus was aware that he was acting as God would do'.[2] It was his character to do so: 'Jesus acts as God acts.'

Historically there can be no doubt that in Jesus' time and in the early Church religious preachers could achieve phenomena which in the judgement of their contemporaries were miracles. The individual stories in the New Testament reflect the consciousness of the narrators that Jesus was performing miracles, even if they expressed this in forms which do not correspond to our understanding of this event. It is certain that in his company they experienced a fullness of life of a kind which immeasurably transcended their daily experiences. In this context the miracles were signs of the 'whole' or complete world of the kingdom of God which was made present in them. Moreover, the proclamation of the nearness of the kingdom of God and the miracles of Jesus belong indissolubly together. That the activity of Jesus which brought healing and restoration and the whole of his lifestyle which freed men and women from distress and misery were part of his ministry is also shown by the fact that Jesus does not just send out his disciples with the command to proclaim his message of the forgiveness of sins and eternal life, in short the message of the kingdom of God, but also enjoins them to heal and restore people (see Mark 3:14–16, 6, 7ff). The people who could experience this salvation from God in Jesus are also themselves called to carry on the work after Jesus, indeed to a still greater degree (John 14:12), in unconditional love for their fellow men and women. The foundation of the lifestyle of Jesus' disciples lies in the lifestyle which Jesus himself followed.[3]

Although it is clear to me that Jesus healed people and that he gives his disciples not only charge but also authority to continue his healing ministry, it is important that we should have a fuller understanding of what Jesus was doing. There are all sorts of wild expectations both unreal and unfaithful that are encouraged the moment people realize that healing should be a feature of the Christian's life.

If we want to encourage the Church to get back to the New Testament, its practice and its life, we should remember that many people were by the age of fifty dead! In Acts we are told that the people were amazed at the healing of a man crippled from birth because he 'was over forty years old' (Acts 4:22)! The fact that in our society many people live well beyond fifty into their seventies and eighties would have seemed positively miraculous to the New Testament Church.

It also needs to be recognized that the healings of Jesus were only temporary remissions. Presumably even Lazarus died again. By healing people and raising them from the dead Jesus was not promising that no one would fall sick and die. Through his miracles Jesus was putting down markers for the kingdom. As far as the people were concerned, especially the sick and the poor, life was ruled by sickness, poverty, disease and death. When Jesus came and healed them it is as if he were saying: 'I know you think that disease and death are the last words on human existence. But I have news for you. There's a new world coming where disease and death will be things of the past.' The healings were powerful signs of this new world. The miraculous healings were Jesus shooting flares into the night sky, lighting up the darkness and promising the dawn of a new age. The miracles of healing were not just signs however; they were the beginnings of the new kingdom breaking in upon and challenging the old order of disease and death. Healings and exorcisms and miracles were the vocabulary of the new kingdom in the language of the old order. So said Jesus in the next chapter: 'If I drive out demons by the Spirit of God, then the kingdom of God has come upon you.' The healings of Jesus were dealing a death blow to the prevailing pessimism that afflicted particularly the sick and the poor. They held out the promise, an optimism of a new future that was already impacting the present. This was Good News for the poor (and disconcerting for those, especially the privileged, who had a vested interest in the continuity of the old order).

The question inevitably arises as to what extent we should see miraculous healings in the Church today. My church in common with many others has an opportunity during the evening communion service for the laying on of hands and prayer for healing. What should we expect on such occasions? John Wimber and others have made a strong plea for 'power evangelism' so that the proclamation of the Good News is associated with the prayer for and the experience of healing. This is advocated on two grounds; firstly, that it is modelled on the evangelistic and healing ministry of Jesus where the two go hand in hand, and secondly that it is a more effective way of persuading the sceptic that there is a God who is there for us. As to whether this method is more effective there is not yet enough statistical evidence to compare other forms of evangelism with that of power evangelism whose evidence is mainly anecdotal. As to being more faithful to the example of Jesus, we need to hear a few caveats.

Where the culture, in which the missionary evangelists are at work, mirrors that of the New Testament then we would expect to repeat the precise model of Jesus' ministry of preaching and healing. In other words, the culture of the New Testament was one where disease and poverty dominated. If we are in a similarly primitive culture where the life of the community is overwhelmed by disease and poverty it seems to me that the practice of Jesus to proclaim the arrival of a new kingdom by physically demonstrating it in miracles of healing is entirely appropriate: 'You think the last words on human existence are disease and poverty. But look to Jesus. He has news for you. Good News. A new world is coming where these will be things of the past. Be healed.' The methods used by Jesus in his culture are exactly right for those ministering in similar cultures. But are they the right models for ministry in a completely different culture?

Not only do people live almost twice as long in our society, the advance in medical science makes our contemporary stories of healing and recovery as miraculous, if not more so, as some of the gospel ones. Severed limbs sewn back on, hearts and lungs transplanted, premature babies incubated and saved. To the eyes of a New Testament believer these would have been miracles. If we consider these to be ultimately from God then they are God's gift every bit as much as the supernatural and spiritual gifts of healing. When we pray and give thanks for healing today we include in the answers to those prayers the providence of God in modern medicine. This is a biblical insight. When, for example, Jesus mixes a paste out of saliva and earth and applies it to a man's eyes it was because such a potion was thought to possess medicinal properties. When, to give another example, the letter of James specifies that the elders of the Church should pray over the sick, 'and anoint him with oil in the name of the Lord' (5:14) it was because oil was regarded as a medicine. In other words, take the medicine and say your prayers.

Translating New Testament practice into the twenty-first century means receiving chemotherapy as a gift from God in the name of the Lord praying that by the power of God's spirit healing will come to you. For the Christian following the ways of the early Church and the example of Jesus it is not a matter of prayer or medicine but both prayer and medicine.

In common with many in the pastoral ministry I have prayed in faith with the Church that God would heal people who are seriously ill. I have seen a few healed and live beyond a pessimistic prognosis. I have seen most die 'in sure and certain hope of the resurrection to eternal life through our Lord Jesus Christ'. Of course, the question always presses in as to why some should be healed and others not. You hear stories from other parts of the world of the most extraordinary miracles. Asia, Africa, South America seem awash with stories of healing.

And in those countries the gospel is being preached, people are responding, the Churches are growing and the kingdom is coming with power and glory. There is no way of checking these stories but even allowing for some exaggeration there's no doubt that the preaching of the gospel is accompanied by healings as it was in the ministry of Jesus. Comparisons with those Churches can lead us to question whether we have the faith sufficient for these things to happen today in our own culture.

While not wanting to evade the challenge of having more faith in God I want to return to the point about the relationship of the culture of the New Testament to the culture of wherever the Church is present. It is clear that in Asia, Africa and South America there are many societies whose deprivation and poverty make them more akin to the conditions of New Testament culture. In such communities where disease and death are the last word on human existence the preaching of the gospel might be demonstrated with healings that challenge the old order and proclaim the in-coming of a new world, a new age, God's kingdom. However, in the northern and western hemispheres of this globe the culture is very different. Disease and death are by no means the last word on human existence. Indeed, the latter of these two words is hardly ever mentioned. There has never been so much health care available in this part of the world. Never in the history of the human family have people had so much access to health care. Never before has health been a political issue. The advances in medical science, however, have not satisfied the thirst for health; on the contrary, it has lead to people having even greater expectations to the point that death, which was once seen as natural, is now considered to be a failure by doctors!

The gift of God to this culture is not healing (we already have it in miraculous abundance by comparison with the New Testament) but how to die well. It is the dread of death that grips our people. The gospel, the Good News, for our culture is not how to postpone death even further but how to face its inevitable beckoning.

Indeed, it is the absence of an eternal perspective that has led us to be so obsessed with hanging onto our existence on earth for dear life. We make a cult of youthfulness and despise the process of growing old. Glossy magazines hold before us the holy icons of this new age, pictures of goddesses, women in their sixties without a wrinkle to crease their ageless faces; jogging and aerobics are the rituals; shell suits and trainers are the vestments. Vitamins and fibre are the sacraments of this new religion.

Good news for this culture is that there is life to be lived beyond the grave. However, to the young, the healthy and the energetic the mention of death is bad news. Mortality is an uncomfortable thought for those who want to stay forever young. This is why in our society it is often the old who find their way to Church, for in spite of medical advances age does eventually become the tamer of lions. Once you have been brought face to face with the finiteness of life and have been stung by the sting of death amongst friends and family, your ears begin to open to the news that there is more of life to be experienced beyond the grave.

When we look at the spectrum of Jesus' teaching, his life, death and resurrection, and examine its relevance to life at the end of the twentieth century in the West, it is fair to conclude that it is on the subject of death and not healing that people need to hear the Good News of Jesus Christ.

The ultimate healing comes through our dying which is the paradise of the Revelation to St John:

Then I saw a new heaven and a new earth, for the first heaven and the first earth had passed away, and there was no longer any sea. I saw the Holy City, the new Jerusalem, coming down out of heaven from God, prepared as a bride beautifully dressed for her husband. And I heard a loud voice from the throne saying, 'Now the dwelling of God is with men, and he will live with them. They will be his people, and God himself will be with them and be their God. He will wipe every tear from their eyes. There will be no more death or mourning or crying or pain, for the old order of things has passed away.'

Revelation (21:1-4)

The anticipation of heaven is the most powerful sustenance in our movement towards death. A moving example of this comes from the life of Alison Dain whose father Bishop Jack Dain encouraged me to write this chapter shortly after her death in April 1993. In his funeral address the Revd David Prior said of Alison:

But in particular, I feel it right to share with you the largely hidden experiences of the last eight or nine months, because I believe this will help us all face up to our own death and our own dying. There were four stages, all eloquently described in her journal. The first I have called – and she called – *the struggle*: August and September 1992, as she wrestled to come to terms with the possible prognosis. Next came *the darkness*: starting in later October/November/December . . . deep darkness, when all seemed very bleak. In those dark times she longed and prayed that she would be able to discover and share 'the treasure of darkness' – a biblical phrase that meant a great deal to her.

The third stage came in January and February this year. She called it *the golden period*. She had made it her goal to be always 'going for gold'. These weeks were times when the feelings of joy, peace and hope returned and filled her. Then, in March, came *the anticipation* when she wrote: 'I am looking forward to death.' She added: 'I feel much more ready to go than to stay. Why should I be reluctant for heaven?'

About this time she actually said: 'If I were given a promise of healing, it would now be a disappointment. I'm ready and at peace about it all.'

It is in such a testimony that we see the goodness of the message of Jesus Christ and its relevance for our death-dreading culture. Healing this side of the grave is only a postponement of death, 'a disappointment', healing through dying and rising with Christ is the hope that God lays before us.

> Therefore my heart is glad and my tongue rejoices:
> my body also will rest secure,
> because you will not abandon me to the grave,
> nor will you let your Holy One see decay.
> You have made known to me the path of life;
> you will fill me with joy in your presence,
> with eternal pleasures at your right hand.

(Psalm 16:9–11)

8

The Authority of Jesus to Give Life

After Jesus said this, he looked towards heaven and prayed:
    Father, the time has come. Glorify your Son, that your Son
may glorify you. For you granted him authority over all
people that he might give eternal life to all those you have
given him. Now this is eternal life: that they may know you,
the only true God, and Jesus Christ, whom you have sent. I
have brought you glory on earth by completing the work you
gave me to do. And now, Father, glorify me in your presence
with the glory I had with you before the world began.
                                                    (John 17:1–5)

The claim of Jesus to have the authority to give eternal life is
surely one of the most extraordinary statements ever to have
been uttered by a human being. In recording it St John is setting
before the reader an unequivocal expression of the divine
nature of Jesus. By human standards it is a preposterous claim.
Its very extravagance leads some commentators to doubt that
Jesus ever said it and to conclude that others must have put
these words into his mouth. But such an interpretation solves
nothing. It only shifts the focus of the question. If it is difficult to
imagine a human being making such a claim for himself it is also
difficult to imagine someone else making up such an extraordinary speech and putting it on his lips. To attribute those
words to someone places upon the writer a heavy responsibility.
No one with any integrity, with any sense of the holy could
lightly write such an exceptional thing! The author of John's

Gospel is concerned with the great issues of darkness and light, judgement and healing, sin and forgiveness, death and life. The images of Jesus which he paints so deftly of the Good Shepherd, the Light, the Vine, the Bread, the Door, the Way, the Truth, the Life, are dramatic pictures of salvation. Here is an author of integrity intensely aware of the conflict between good and evil, destruction and peace. No one handling such serious themes about the world and its predicament could write about the person of Jesus in this way if he were not possessed of a conviction that he did indeed say such things and have 'the authority to give eternal life'. If that conviction is without foundation then everything else that he writes is as secure as a sandcastle built on the shore of an incoming tide. If these spoken words of Jesus, which reveal his character as surely as music when it is played reveals the true nature of the notation on the sheet, were indeed uttered by him, then they bring us face to face with a man who spoke and lived like no other person. His claim is not that he will show the seeker the way to life eternal but that this very life is his gift to bestow.

There are several words in the Gospels which are rendered in English by the word 'life'. Here John uses the word *zoe* as opposed to *bios*. The latter describes the biological and physical aspect of living, e.g. the life that you live for approximately seventy years, the life that you sustain with food and drink, the life that you lead selfishly or kindly. This life (*bios*) owes its existence to God but is limited to the body. The word John uses here and in John 10:10 'I have come that they may have life, and have it to the full' has an altogether different meaning. *Zoe* is the life that describes the very being of God himself e.g.: 'For as the Father has life (*zoe*) in himself, so he has granted the Son to have life (*zoe*) in himself' (John 5:26). *Zoe* is the life that emanates from God which is the source of all creation, physical and spiritual. *Bios* is the life *that* we live; *Zoe* is the life *by which* we live.

St John defines this life of God in three ways. It is given to

Jesus to give such life; it is eternal; and it is to know God and Jesus Christ.

In books on spirituality and evangelism there is frequent reference to the concept of 'new life'. People are encouraged to find 'new life' in God or 'new life' in a personal relationship with Jesus Christ'. Yet there is no such concept in the Gospels. Jesus never speaks of 'new life'. The New Testament speaks about a new covenant, a new person, a new creation, a new self, a new birth, a new earth but never about a 'new life'. The only word that is ever used to describe more fully 'life' apart from Hebrews (7:16) where life is referred to as indestructible or indissoluble, is the adjective 'eternal'. (In Acts 5:20 the mention of 'new' is an unwarranted intrusion into the translation; in Romans 6:4 Paul writes about walking in 'the newness (the freshness) of life').

To talk about '*new* life' through a relationship with God is to suggest that there is some sort of life to be lived apart from him. This is something that the world has always wanted to believe. It has searched for that life in so many dark places and continues to do so. Yet without God there simply is no life. There is existence, there is sensation, there is seeing, hearing, touching, smelling and tasting. There is *bios*. But without God, separated from God, there is no *zoe*. When, however, we enter into a relationship with God that life flows over us and through us and we are immersed like a sponge in water. That Life, because it originates with the everlasting God is thereby eternal Life. It goes on from age to age. It is indestructible and indissoluble because God is such. Eternal is, therefore, the adjective which is used exclusively of Life in the New Testament.

The Life of God is the gift which he offers to the whole world through his filial emissary Jesus Christ. The famous passages of John's Gospel are the motifs in the symphony of divine life:

God so loved the world that he gave his one and only Son, that whoever believes in him shall not perish but have eternal life. (3:16)

In him was life, and that life was the light of men. (1:4)

Whoever hears my word and believes him who sent me has eternal life; he has crossed over from death to life. (5:24)

I am the resurrection and the life. He who believes in me will live; even though he dies; and whoever loves and believes in me will never die. (11:25)

Eternal life is not just a future prospect. It is a present reality. It is the Life that is lived now in communion with the eternal God. This Life will go on forever not because the person who receives it is inherently immortal but because the giver and his gift are eternal.

Pastorally this insight is of immense value not least in the chapel of a crematorium or standing by a grave committing the dead 'in sure and certain hope of the resurrection to eternal life'. In such moments it is often difficult to grasp the continuity of a person's life. The smoke from the crematorium and the dark cavity of the grave emphasize the destructibility of the body. Dust to dust, ashes to ashes. When the body has been reduced to such elements it is hard to conceive of that which has been destroyed by fire or decayed in the earth having an eternal destiny. If in a funeral service we concentrate too much on the deceased by never going beyond the traditional eulogy then it becomes all the more difficult to glimpse eternity. The focus of our thoughts, however thankful and full of praise, is the loved one whose body we see being committed to the process of decomposition. We may try and encourage belief in eternity and a life after the crematorium but what we see happening to the coffin with our eyes makes a greater impact on us and a more indelible mark than what we hear about the dead person's virtues.

The eternal life of the believer is not in the end about imagining his immortality or that of his loved ones. Eternal life is seeing that God 'in whom we move and have our being' is the Eternal One and that it is he who goes on forever. What

Christians celebrate, or ought to, at a funeral is not the immortality of the soul however virtuous but the Eternal God in whom we will as 'spiritual bodies' continue to move and have our being. Our eternal life is through being bound to the Eternal One. It is the grandeur of God and not the greatness of man that is the source of our confidence and the inspiration of our hope of life eternal.

There is a poignant episode in Lord Hailsham's autobiography *A Sparrow's Flight* when he meets with Winston Churchill for the last time before his death. Churchill enquires of Hailsham whether he believes in life after death:

> Long silence.
>   'Do you believe in the afterlife?'
>   'Why, yes, Winston, I do.'
>   'H'mm.'
>   Long silence.
>   'You remember, Winston, when you were at the bottom of that coal-mine on the run as an escaped prisoner of war?'
>   'Yes.'
>   'You said you prayed for help and it always came.'
>   'H'mm.' It was evident that his soul was clad in dust and ashes.
>   'And remember, Winston, that all over the world millions of men and women who remember what you have done will always bless your name. And I am one.'
>   'H'mm.'
>   Long silence.
>   We parted warmly. It was the last time I ever saw him alive. As I went back in the taxi to my home in Roehampton, I cried silently to myself at the dark moment of despair which had befallen this giant among men.

Belief in the afterlife although it preoccupies many souls, especially as they draw near to death, is a sub-Christian idea. It suggests that you live, you die, and you may live again. The New

Testament picture of Life Eternal is more embracing and more reassuring. The Life of God which infuses the believer, the truster in God, is everlasting. Once this Life, this indissoluble and indestructible Life, has taken hold of our whole being we are secure for eternity. Nothing can destroy you . . . none can snatch you out of the Father's grip . . . nothing can separate you from God's love.

In this passage from John's Gospel we hear Jesus claiming the authority to give such Life Eternal in the here and now. Giving Life is the prerogative of God. The Father authorizes his Son to bestow this gift. The secret to experiencing Life is to 'know you, the only true God, and Jesus Christ whom you have sent'. The word 'know' speaks of an intimate and immediate relationship where there is communion between the knower and the known. As in all intimate relationships there is a time to keep silence in each other's presence and a time for speaking. Knowing God and being known by him will mean moments of stillness when we keep wordless company with God and times of endless petition when we pour out our souls. The outcome of such knowing is that we have Life. But how do we know that this Life is ours, that we have been made alive by God?

In his beautiful book *A Matter of Life and Death*[1] Bishop John Taylor explores through a number of evocative stories the signs of being alive to God. 'The essence of that vitality which makes a person . . . really alive is responsiveness, or ability to respond.' When our children wanted to know if the hamsters were just sleeping or dead the simple test was to prod them for a reaction! 'And many a child visiting Madame Tussaud's Waxworks has discovered whether the attendant at the foot of the stairs was alive or not only by asking him a question or poking him in the ribs. Response or non-response is the test.'

And so it is in our relationship with God. The sign of being alive or dead to God is the response or non-response to his love for us in Jesus Christ. The person who is dead, for whom the Life of God is as distant as the Sahara desert from the fjords of Norway, finds himself untouched and uninspired by Jesus Christ.

There is no response to God's love, which leaves him cold and unmoved. On the other hand, the person who has received from Jesus the gift of God's Life finds within himself the stirring of a response – the first expressions of gratitude to God, the desire to follow the example of Jesus, the appetite to be filled with a sense of God's peace, a longing to be deeply affected by the love of God, a child-like enjoyment in sharing with God both the delights and the frustrations. These are some of the signs that we are being transfused with the Life of God. These are the signs of coming alive and being enthused with divine Life.

John Taylor tells a moving story set in a nursing home for old people. The residents sit in their wheelchairs half-paralysed, half-dead. One day a ballet dancer is brought in who dances to the sound of familiar and beautiful classical music. Soon the residents who have hardly ever moved a limb begin to tap, some with their hands, some with their feet. The room comes alive as the dancer transfuses the residents with her own vitality and life. John Taylor singles this out not just as a remarkable therapy but: 'As an instance of the effect of the really alive upon the half-dead or upon lifeless situations. And, in particular, it throws light on the impact of Jesus Christ upon his contemporaries.'[2]

Although Jesus has 'authority over all people that he might give them eternal life' not everybody then or now was willing to receive his gift. The argument of the universalist who believes that God's love will embrace all and melt the frozen hearts of the rebellious seems to me weak at this point. It is based on the optimistic view that when all come face to heart with divine love they will soften and repent. But many people encountered God's compassion in the face of Jesus and although some turned to him in faith others resolutely set their face against his.

Kenneth Clark, the art historian who made the celebrated television series *Civilization*, wrote of a religious experience he had in the Church of San Lorenzo in Venice.

I can only say that for a few minutes my whole being was irradiated by a kind of heavenly joy, far more intense than anything I had known before. This state of mind lasted for several months, and, wonderful though it was, it posed an awkward problem in terms of action. My life was far from blameless: I would have to reform. My family would think I was going mad, and perhaps after all, it was a delusion, for I was in every way unworthy of receiving such a flood of grace. Gradually the effect wore off, and I made no effort to retain it. I think I was right; I was too deeply embedded in the world to change course. But that I had 'felt the finger of God' I am quite sure.[3]

Clark's candour especially about being 'too deeply embedded in the world to change course' puts one in mind of the rich young man who enquired of Jesus: 'Good teacher, what must I do to inherit eternal life?' The answer, like Clark's experience of 'the finger of God', was too demanding in spite of the riches that it promised. Neither man at that particular moment in their existence felt able to submit to the authority of Jesus to give them Life Eternal.

Those who submit to the authority of Jesus and receive from him the assurance of eternal life are caught up in the prayer of Jesus that they should become, even like God himself, holy. Our journey on earth becomes a pilgrimage towards heaven. While we travel in the company of Christ our lives and characters change. Jesus is our example and inspiration. Through this transformation we begin to look like people who would enjoy the company of heaven. Without such a change heaven would be an alien and foreign land for us. J. C. Ryle captured such a thought in his classic book *Holiness*:

No man can possibly be happy in a place where he is not in his element, and where all around him is not congenial to his tastes, habits and character. When an eagle is happy in an iron cage, when a sheep is happy in the water, when an owl is happy in the blaze of noonday sun, when a fish is happy on the dry land – then, and not till then, will I admit that the unsanctified man could be happy in heaven.

9

The Authority of Jesus to Teach

'Watch out for false prophets. They come to you in sheep's clothing, but inwardly they are ferocious wolves. By their fruit you will recognize them. Do people pick grapes from thornbushes, or figs from thistles? Likewise every good tree bears good fruit, but a bad tree bears bad fruit. A good tree cannot bear bad fruit, and a bad tree cannot bear good fruit. Every tree that does not bear good fruit is cut down and thrown into the fire. Thus, by their fruit you will recognize them.

'Not everyone who says to me "Lord, Lord", will enter the kingdom of heaven, but only he who does the will of my Father who is in heaven. Many will say to me on that day, "Lord, Lord, did we not prophesy in your name, and in your name drive out demons and perform many miracles?"

'Then I will tell them plainly, "I never knew you. Away from me, you evildoers?"

'Therefore everyone who hears these words of mine and puts them into practice is like a wise man who built his house on the rock. The rain came down, the streams rose, and the winds blew and beat against that house; yet it did not fall, because it had its foundation on the rock. But everyone who hears these words of mine and does not put them into practice is like a foolish man who built his house on sand. The rain came down, the streams rose, and the winds blew and beat against the house, and it fell with a great crash.'

When Jesus had finished saying these things, the crowds were amazed at his teaching, because he taught as one who

had authority, and not as their teachers of the law.
(Matthew 7:15–29)

Jesus taught with authority. There was a charismatic quality to his teaching that was lacking in the official teachers. Jesus had no education other than that which he received as a boy in the synagogue. This should not be underestimated. Along with every other young male he was taught there to read and write and to learn the Scriptures by rote. Although not formally trained as a rabbi he taught in a rabbinic style, engaging his audience in dialogue and cajoling them with stories. This was how he was taught and, in turn, how he himself taught his followers. The Sermon on the Mount is a good example of this. It is full of epigrams, pictures and parables.

The parable was one of his principal tools in teaching. Analysing a parable can empty it of its power in the same way that trying to explain a joke can render it as flat as stale lemonade! Nevertheless, it is important to be aware of the qualities that make the parable such an engaging method of communication.

Many of the stories Jesus tells are funny with larger than life caricatures of clergy swallowing camels, personal debts amounting to five times the country's total tax revenue, planks of wood jutting out of the eye and fathers setting down before ravenous children meals of scorpions and snakes! Humour gets people laughing, relaxing; it makes them receptive: both the teacher and his message become accessible. Above all it makes connection with the real world because although there is a serious and tragic dimension to life there is also an absurd and comic side. Jesus captures and expresses both in his teaching about the kingdom of God.

The stories that Jesus tells have characters and plots that people can identify with even though they might not agree with the sentiment. Eulogizing a Samaritan in the presence of orthodox Jews was like going to Baghdad and praising the Americans. People were on the edge of their seats listening to Jesus' stories.

He told them about the kingdom of God in pictures and stories of their own culture that they could connect with and enter into.

As with every good story-teller Jesus mastered the art of the surprise. Indeed, it has been suggested that if you want to know the meaning or meanings of a parable you tell the story until you come to that point when you could add 'surprise, surprise!' Take the well-known but inaccurately named parable of the Prodigal son as an example. (It is, in fact, known by Jesus as the story of 'The man who had two sons'; from the outset we might expect to find at least three points!) We know from the culture of his day that for a younger son to demand his inheritance was in effect to say to his father 'I wish you were dead'. That's the first surprise in the story. The second surprise is that when the younger son has enough of the low life and decides to return home he not only finds his father waiting but actually running towards him with arms open wide; in his culture there was a tradition that the heavily-robed nobility did not run in public, in the same way that in our society there has been a convention never to film the Queen running or eating in public. The third surprise in the story is left hanging in the air by the story-teller. The elder brother's understandable pique is challenged by his father. But the question which is unresolved is 'did the elder brother go in and join the party?' The story leaves us guessing. At each of these three points of surprise the parable engages us in the lives and actions of the three key players: the younger son, the father and the elder brother. It is more than the story of a prodigal son. It is a story that makes us ask questions not just about the characters but ultimately about ourselves as we see in them and their relationships aspects of our own lives reflected.

The power of this story came home to me when I worked as an audio-visual producer. I had recorded Kenneth Williams telling a modern version of this story. As I was working in the studio at the tape recorder, wielding my razor blade editing the tape, I was being watched by a friend who had dropped in to

see me. He was in his final year reading Theology. I finished the
edit, mixed the music and played it through. I turned round to
get my friend's reaction. His head was in his hands. He looked
up, tears in his eyes. 'What's wrong . . .?' 'I've just seen . . . I'm
the elder brother . . .' As he lost himself in the story so he found
himself. He came face to face with aspects of his own life and
story. He saw the resentments, jealousies and bitternesses of the
elder brother like a mirror to his own. That's how parables
work.

The parable is more than an illustration. It is not simply the
sugar-coating of a theological pill that the teacher wants his
followers to swallow. Kenneth Bailey, who has done much in
recent years to throw light on the meaning of the parable by
understanding the Palestinian culture in which Jesus lived, helps
us appreciate the true value of the parable. Quoting Manson,
the New Testament scholar, he writes:

> Illustrations will not be parables in the sense that the parables
> of the New Testament are parables. They (illustrations) are
> merely the embellishment of something else, namely the
> chain of logical reasoning; they are the sugar-coating on
> the theological pill.
>
> The true parable, on the other hand, is not an illustration to
> help one through a theological discussion; it is rather a mode
> of religious experience. It belongs to the same order of things
> as altar and sacrifice, prayer, the prophetic vision, and the
> like. It is a datum for theology, not a by-product. It is a way
> in which religious faith is attained and, so far as it can be,
> transmitted from one person to another. It is not a crutch for
> limping intellects, but a spur to religious insight; its object is
> not to provide simple theological instruction, but to produce
> living religious faith.

In Bailey's own words: 'a parable is not an illustration but is a
mode of theological speech used to evoke a response . . . The
listener is challenged by the telling of a parable to respond'.

The story engages the emotions as well as the mind; it stirs the imagination and challenges the will. That is why the testimony of someone else's experience of God can be so moving and lead the listener to faith. The response to a parable can be negative as well as positive. Jesus certainly used parables as a Galilean rabbi to help people see and enter into the kingdom of God. But he also used parables like a prophet of the Old Testament whose symbolic actions and words confronted people with the judgement of God. This is the significance of the quotation in Mark 4 from Isaiah 6 when, explaining his use of parables, Jesus says:

> He told them. 'The secret of the kingdom of God has been given to you. But to those on the outside everything is said in parables so that,
>> "they may be ever seeing but never perceiving,
>> and ever hearing but never understanding,
>> otherwise they might turn and be forgiven." '
>
> (Mark 4:11–12)

Jesus was a prophet as well as a rabbi. His stories, told to vast crowds of both protagonists and antagonists, evoked different responses. Those who were being drawn through him into the kingdom of God found in his stories the secret of forgiveness and *shalom*; those whose hearts were calloused to the demands of God's rule over their lives, especially in the way that it was expressed through the life, actions and teaching of Jesus, found his stories of the kingdom of God a stumbling block. The parables of Jesus confirmed his opponents in their opposition to him. In resisting him they deprived themselves of the spiritual insight and understanding that could have led them to repentance, forgiveness and *shalom*. The parables of Jesus the prophet brought upon them the judgement of God for their culpable hardness of heart and spiritual blindness. Matthew points up this prophetic character to Jesus' parables when, after Jesus had told the disturbing story of 'the Parable of the Tenants' he adds: 'When the chief priests and the Pharisees heard Jesus' parables, *they knew he was talking about them*. They looked for a way to arrest him, but they were afraid of the crowd because the people held that he was a *prophet*' (Matthew 21:45-46, my italics).

It is significant that Matthew clusters this and several other parables after the challenge to the authority of Jesus when he was teaching in the Temple (21:23-27). Jesus skilfully evades the issue by typically turning the tables on them with a question about the authority of John's ministry of baptism. As with John, the central issue is his status and calling as a prophet. All could recognize that Jesus the Galilean had no formal education to qualify him as a rabbi. The question, however, was 'is this man a prophet?', for which educational qualifications were not a prerequisite. If the authority for his teaching was because he was a prophet then ultimately that authority was from God whose mouth-piece the prophet is. The opponents of Jesus were on the horns of a dilemma. The people had already sensed that Jesus not only taught with greater authority than their educated teachers but that he was also a prophet, someone through whom God had already begun to address them about the kingdom of heaven.

The way Jesus used story as both a rabbi and a prophet is an object lesson in communication which the Church today would do well to heed. A contributory factor to the Church's alienation from contemporary culture lies in its inability to use the language and symbols of ordinary people. This was a mistake that Jesus was never guilty of. It has often struck me that if we send people as missionaries to another culture we prepare them with, for example, language training, cultural awareness, skills in cross-cultural communication; yet we plunge people into mission in our own country with very little regard to and preparation for the appropriate means of communication. We live in an audio-visual culture which means that the mass of the population think visually rather than in abstract concepts. In fact, the medium of television—which the average person spends eight years of their life watching—does two things in our culture; it is a medium of story-telling and stimulates the appetite for story so that the schedules are saturated to the point of a foaming lather with soap operas; and it makes people impatient with abstract concepts hence the poor viewing figures for programmes that deal principally with ideas. This is not the place for a debate about the merits and demerits of the media in contemporary society. Colin Morris in *God in a Box*, Wesley Carr in *Ministry and the Media*, and even Malcolm Muggeridge's *Christ and the Media* offer excellent perspectives on this subject. However much we may lament the constraints of mission in and to an audio-visual culture I want to highlight a few principles about communicating the Christian faith.

I was running a course in the parish on teaching the Christian faith to young people and was making the point that we needed to avoid peddling abstract concepts and to choose, instead, stories and pictures. I drew attention to that most popular of abstract concepts in theology, namely 'God is love', and asked the group how many times they thought this occurred in the Bible. I offered some guidance and asked whether it was over or under five hundred times. Instantly a man shouted out 'five thousand times'. He and the whole group were surprised to learn that it occurs only twice in the whole Bible; never in the Gospels and only in the letters of John. As far as we know, the concept was never on the lips of Jesus. It is possible that he never said such a thing! The Gospels, the parables, the Bible are full of stories about how God loves us (and often in the most surprising ways) but they do not set much store by reiterating the abstract proposition 'God is love'.

That is not to say that there is no place in theology and teaching for the abstract concept. But to a Church that fails to communicate with ordinary people, partly because it does not speak their language, it is a useful corrective to note that the Scriptures and Jesus himself provide other models for showing the world that God loves us. The story, the picture, the parable and the simile are the methods of Jesus.

The tension between images and concepts is illustrated by John McQuarrie:

Although the concrete imagery of kingship, fatherhood and so on cannot be superseded in the actual life of religion, in prayer and liturgy for instance (who ever addressed a prayer to necessary being?); and although the strongly personalist and even anthropomorphic language serves to keep before the worshipper that sense of affinity with the divine being which we have seen to be essential to belief in God and which it is the business of religion to encourage and enhance, reflective members of the religious community have looked for ways of expressing theism that would be more satisfying intellectually. In general, they have tried to move away from images to concepts and to express theism as a philosophical doctrine.[2]

McQuarrie accurately describes the move 'away from images to concepts'. Herein lies the Church's problem. In order to communicate with ordinary people in an audio-visual culture it must learn to move again *back* from the concepts to *images* that people can see, understand and believe in.

The Church faces a crisis of communication because through enshrining all that it knows about God in abstract concepts it denies the keys of the kingdom of God to those people who see and understand through pictures and parables. (And we are not talking simply about children; Jesus told his stories to adult audiences.)

When St Paul, in that famous passage in 1 Corinthians 13, reflected on one day knowing fully and being known fully by God he compared our present experience of knowing God to looking through a glass. The classic rendering of this text in the Authorised Version says: 'For now we see through a glass, darkly.' But in the Greek there is no mention of 'darkly' or 'dimly' (RSV) or 'poor reflection' (NIV) or 'puzzling reflections' (NEB) or 'dim reflection' (JB). What St Paul confesses is that as yet we see through a mirror *'in a riddle'* (enigma); in other words, in stories, parables, simile, allegory and metaphor. The point he is making is that it is through the enigmatic medium of images and pictures that we begin to relate to God. The way that we know God is through pictures and images such as Father, Shepherd, King. These images enable us to relate to God by conjuring up in our imagination further pictures of ourselves as children, sheep and loyal subjects. These and other such icons are the means of grace, of knowing and being known by God. To those who might object by saying that the writings of St Paul are full of abstract concepts the point must be made that his letters are in fact full of pictures such as the athletes, the farmer, the soldier's armour, prisoners in chains, acquittal in the law-courts, the redemption of slaves. These biblical images enable us to see ourselves in relation to God and are indispensable to our spirituality.

The problem is that so much theological education to which prospective ministers are subjected pays little attention to this dominical method of conceiving and communicating the kingdom of God in pictures. 'To express theism as a philosophical doctrine'[3] takes priority over all other considerations so that the average ordained person comes out of college and into a parish, or the average lay preacher comes out of his training course and into a pulpit, and is quite unable to communicate! Their sermons creak with abstract concepts and their audiences give the appearance of listening while finding more interesting things for their imaginations to dwell on! Any use made of the story is usually some inconsequential and light-hearted anecdote to warm up the congregation at the beginning. It is seldom integral to the sermon. My concern is not that we should abandon abstract concepts for these are indeed important in developing a coherent and systematic doctrine; my plea is that the story is of equal value in knowing God; that the story is the method used by Jesus; that in this audio-visual culture with its appetite for story we could do no better in our teaching and evangelism than to emulate the example of Jesus the teacher.

The problem is that the teacher's search for authority often leads him to find it in his education. Thus he makes his audience aware of his great learning by long words, difficult concepts and erudite quotations. There's nothing wrong with any of these three features as the reader of this book may well have judged! But if that is thought to be the focus of his authority then I think he has a problem. To return to the example of Jesus, it is significant that when his audiences compared him with the formally-educated teachers they noted that it was Jesus who had the authority.

Indeed, it was the endowment of authority that singled him out from the others. That authority flowed from his relationship with God and not from his education.

John McIntyre identifies three periods in the Western Church's history.[4] The first, iconolatry when the Church fell into the trap of actually worshipping the images through which it was to see God; the second, iconoclasm, when for political and ecclesiastical as well as theological reasons images were destroyed at the Reformation; the third, iconophobia whereby ever since the Church has been wary of images not only in its liturgy but in its theology. This has led to: 'Aniconistic thinking, or imageless thought, as being the norm of theological reflection and articulation.'[5] He argues passionately and persuasively for the re-integration of image and imagination in religion and theology but recognizes that to do so runs counter 'to the theological tides of the ages'. Although a technical book which indulges rightly in its own feast of abstract thinking this is one of the most important books to be written recently on the relationship of theology to the world.

When emphasizing the importance of image and imagination I have often sensed in people a resistance and a fear that somehow this undermines the given-ness of God's revelation through Scripture. My own position is that I believe that biblical images have a primacy in all theological reflection. We need to understand the cultural context of the images which is why the works of Kenneth Bailey are so important. Should these images and stories fail to make an impact on the imagination in the culture where our own mission is located, then we must use our imagination to conjure up other images that tell the same story about knowing and being known by God, about loving and being loved by God. Of course, this is what translators of the Bible have been doing ever since the first translations from the original Hebrew and Greek text:

> A translator of the Bible or indeed of any other ancient text, cannot succeed in his task merely by a transference from one language to another; he must also undertake the transfer from the thought forms and pre-suppositions of the ancient world, from all its mental furnishings to those of the present day.[6]

So, for example, when it comes to describing Jesus as the Lamb of God to an Eskimo who has never in his life set eyes upon a sheep, it is culturally appropriate to visualize him as an innocent and vulnerable seal.

Encouraging the use of image and imagination does not mean that we should be uncritical. It is possible both in our worship and teaching to use too many images or the wrong images or inappropriate images. For a period of a year we experimented at our baptisms with the giving of a lighted candle to the baptized infant. It is a beautiful symbol through which one sees that Jesus is the light of the world and that through him one passes from darkness into light. But after a year's experiment, we (the clergy and the lay leaders) decided to discontinue the practice. What worried us was that the candle was eclipsing the sacrament of baptism. It was the candle that people held onto and cherished and remembered. The dominical sacrament of baptism in water with its symbolic washing away of sin was relegated to a place of secondary importance. It was soon the candle that everybody was asking for. We were conscious that although Jesus saw himself as the light of the world he did not initiate people in to the kingdom of God with lit tapers. He chose a natural element to cleanse the believer symbolically. It has to be said that the church where I am vicar is not candle-orientated and subconsciously this may well have contributed to the decision, although we tried to recognize this influence. It must also be recognized that in other cultural contexts, such as Asian and Hindu areas, the light may be a much more appropriate symbol. I give this example simply to make the point that in our choice of images we should not be uncritical but discerning in what we communicate through the images that we choose.

Choosing the right images demands energy and creativity as well as a lively imagination, yet so often those of us called to teach the Christian faith find all three in short supply. The result is that we resort to clichés and familiar, sterile images. George Orwell in his essay 'Politics and the English language'[7] writes damningly about the staleness of imagery in political writing. His comments serve also as an accurate description of much of the teaching that you hear in the Church today: 'phrases tacked together like the sections of a prefabricated hen-house', 'There is a huge dump of worn-out metaphors which have lost all evocative power', 'By using stale metaphors, similes and idioms you save much mental effort . . .'. Orwell would have made the same comments about sermons! As someone nurtured in and committed to teaching the orthodox faith I find this comment devastatingly accurate: 'Orthodox, of whatever colour, seems to demand a lifeless imitative style, one never finds in them a fresh vivid, home-made turn of speech.'

I am often invited to lead workshops on preaching for clergy and laity. Having made all the above points I've been challenged by those who have been persuaded, as to what they can do about it. I remember one vicar asking passionately: 'What do you do when you've run out of all your stories?' He knew the value of stories, and knew too that although you can preach the same sermon every week to the same congregation and get very little reaction, you can't tell the same story twice! Many preachers get to the end of a sermon in their preparation and, feeling that it is very dry, try to think up illustrations that will get the thing off the page and into the minds of the congregation. Going this extra mile is commendable. But the problem is one of how you begin rather than how you end. Mostly those of us educated to a tertiary level begin with the abstract concept then try to illustrate it. What we need rather to do is to begin by thinking of the concrete image.

> When you think of a *concrete object*, you think wordlessly, and then, if you want to describe the thing you've been *visualizing* you probably hunt about till you find the exact words to fit it. When you think of something abstract, you are more inclined to use words from the start, and unless you make a conscious effort to prevent it, the existing dialect will come rushing in and do the job for you.[8]

For example, if we start with the abstract idea 'God is Love' and continue to dwell on it our minds will soon fill up with other concepts such as forgiveness, compassion, mercy, reconciliation, peace and so on. The ideas will explode easily in our minds like someone tossing a lighted match into a box of bangers. If, on the other hand, we start with a picture then our imaginations, our emotions and our wills, will become engaged as we begin to visualize the scene. For example, if we begin with 'His father saw him and had compassion and ran and embraced him and kissed him' and we then meditate on the picture, the scene will become more vivid in our imaginations. It may recall other scenes and experiences which resonate with the emotions stirred in us by the original picture. When we come to communicating this with others we are more likely 'to hunt about till we find the exact words to fit it'. It is this freshness and originality that I see in the stories of Jesus. They were imaginative means of grace for his audiences who in and through the parables discovered not just the abstract concept 'God is Love' but that God actually loved them like a Good Father and in the most surprising ways.

One of the most engaging modern story-tellers, the late Roald Dahl, offers, by way of a post-script, the ingredients of a good story!

It is essential to think of a strong plot. Work out the basic story before you start writing.

You need a quick beginning. Get right into the story, otherwise people won't go on reading.

You need to amuse your readers. Go for lots of laughs.

Make up some extraordinary and unusual characters. Remember, ordinary people are dull.

Have one or two very bad people in the story – and do them in at the end.

It is important that the hero or heroine must win.

Exaggerate and go overboard. Be daring with everything and when you have done that take it even further and be even more daring and more bizarre. And then go further still . . . [9]

10

The Authority of Jesus to Make Disciples

Then the eleven disciples went to Galilee, to the mountain where Jesus had told them to go. When they saw him, they worshipped him; but some doubted. Then Jesus came to them and said, 'All authority in heaven and on earth has been given to me. Therefore go and make disciples of all nations, baptizing them in the name of the Father and of the Son and of the Holy Spirit, and teaching them to obey everything I have commanded you. And surely I will be with you always, to the very end of the age.

(Matthew 28:16–20)

Throughout the writing of these essays on the authority of Jesus I have wondered whether I should have opened with this chapter. This is the last mention of authority (*exousia*) in the Gospel of Matthew yet in many ways everything about Jesus' life and ministry, death and resurrection flow from this declaration on the mountain in Galilee.

'All authority in (*en*) heaven and on (*epi*) earth has been given to me. Therefore . . .' The source of the authority of Jesus is in heaven with the Father and the area over which it is to be exercised is the earth. Just as a judge has authority vested in him by the state so he exercises that authority over the court. The state is the source, the court is the arena. And the effectual process of exercising that authority is what we might call his power. So the source of the authority of Jesus is heaven; the arena is the earth; the process is his power.

Jesus is an authoritative and powerful person. He does not lord it over people. On the contrary he exercises his authority powerfully as a servant. This is his character not only at his first coming but also at his second coming (see Luke 12:37 for a picture of Jesus coming again as a *servant* Lord). The character of Jesus who is 'the same yesterday, today and forever' is that of a deacon. He is the image of the Deacon God who in the vision to St John is revealed as the God who continues to minister to his people by wiping away the tears from their eyes. Jesus exercises his authority and power on his knees. The only time that he ever refers to himself as 'Lord' is when he is washing away the dirt from his disciples' feet.

A friend of mine recalls being taught how to box by a champion boxer who bore in his face and his ears all the marks of his fights. Although retired he was still a man of great but controlled strength. As he coached these young boys he was as gentle and as constrained as a lioness with her cubs. The power was there but suffused in a gentle meekness as he brought the best out of his fledglings. Thus Jesus channelled his power into serving and enabling and empowering his own.

The siting of this great declaration and commission is significant. Jesus directs the disciples to go to Galilee some eighty miles north of Jerusalem. Why? Maybe he wanted to take them back to where it had all begun. Maybe he wanted them to realize how far they had come in those three years since they met on the shores of Lake Galilee. As far as Matthew was concerned, Galilee was a place with a particular reputation:

'Land of Zebulun and land of Naphtali,
the way to the sea, along the Jordan,
Galilee of the Gentiles –
the people living in darkness
have seen a great light;
on those living in the land of the

shadow of death
a light has dawned.'

(Matthew 4:15–16)

(Note that the Greek word *Éthne* can be translated as Gentiles, nations or races.) Galilee of the Gentiles, of the nations of the other races, was a borderland, a place of many immigrants. As with all countries with immigrants there was a degree of inter-marriage so that to the orthodox Jew it was a region that was less than Kosher. Yet in the Gospel of Matthew it is a place that is held in affection. It is the safe haven where Joseph and his family escape to on their return from Egypt. It is the place that marks the beginning of Jesus' public ministry and where Jesus calls out his disciples. This dubious region with its impure stock, its half-castes and mixture of races is where Jesus begins and ends his earthly ministry.

Commentators often stress that Matthew's Gospel was writ-ten for the Jewish community. There is a great emphasis on Jesus fulfilling the prophesies of the Old Testament. However no author seeking to commend himself and his message to the Jewish audience would give such a high and favourable profile to Galilee, the region of other races unless Jesus had made this a central issue of his ministry. It adds weight to the historicity of this last passage in Matthew's Gospel that the episode is specifically located in Galilee. No one would make that up if he wished to sell his story to the Jews.

Why then does Jesus direct his disciples to 'Galilee of the other races'? And why does Matthew record it? As a border-land Galilee was a frontier region between God's people and the rest of the world. By taking them to Galilee's mountain he was showing them their destiny: 'make disciples of all races'. As they looked into the horizon they were beginning to grasp that the God of Abraham, Isaac and Moses who had promised and given them a land of their own was in reality a God without frontiers. In eschewing Jerusalem and choosing Galilee Jesus was breaking with the tradition of the past where it was anticipated that all the nations of the world would come to Jerusalem for salvation. Now they were to go out from Jerusalem, the place of crucifixion and resurrection, and to Galilee of the Gentiles and beyond Galilee in order to make disciples of all races. Up until that moment mission had been centripetal, focussed on Jerusalem. Now it was centrifugal, scattering the seed to the ends of the earth, the earth over which Christ himself exercised his heaven-given authority.

In Galilee Jesus had already demonstrated the love of God for the outsider. Now in this moment he declares that love for Galilee with all its different races and for all the peoples beyond. This is a surprising end to a Gospel for the Jews! Although, on reflection, it is consonant with the opening of the Gospel which has as the first worshippers of Jesus the men from the East.

Jesus' attitude to the non-Jewish races is most powerfully articulated in the episode of the cleansing of the Temple. I have argued a different interpretation in another book *Falling into Grace*.[1] Most commentators on this event concentrate on the commercialism of the traders and its inappropriateness in the Temple Courts. But to concentrate on this point is to overlook something of greater significance. It is not so much *what* they were doing but *where* they were doing it. The outer courts of the Temple were set aside for the Gentiles, the non-Jewish races to draw close to God. By taking the courts over the traders were robbing the Gentiles of their place and their opportunity of coming close to God. This point comes through by translating the verse in a slightly different but legitimate way: 'My house shall be called a house of prayer for *all races*' (Mark 11:17). The crime of the people was turning the courts into a 'den of robbers' and so depriving the other races of their place of prayer.

The point is further substantiated by the context in Isaiah from which Jesus quotes the verse.

Let no foreigner who has joined himself to the Lord say, 'The Lord will surely exclude me from his people' . . . and foreigners who bind themselves to the Lord to serve him, to love the name of the Lord and to worship him . . . those I will bring to my holy mountain and give them joy in my house of prayer . . . for my house will be called a house of prayer for *all races*. (Isaiah 56)

What the Temple authorities had done in giving permission to the traders to use the Temple Courts was to 'exclude' the other races and deny the promise of God that the Jewish Temple should be a place of prayer not only for Jews but for Gentiles, for other races. That is why Jesus was angry. It was the racism that kept out the other peoples that filled Jesus, like Jeremiah, with 'the fury of the Lord'.

To add to this point further, the quotation from Jeremiah about the Temple being turned into a 'den of robbers' (7:11) is directly associated with the neglect of widows and orphans and the oppression of the foreigner by the people of Judah (7:6). Racism is endemic in all societies. The Jewish people have in their history been more its victims than its perpetrators. Yet a racism that deprives others of drawing near to God is something that Jesus would naturally set his face against. And just as the Temple failed to be 'a house of prayer for all races', I wonder how much the Church of England has also failed to be a 'house of prayer for all races'? I sense that we, like the Temple authorities, may also come under the judgement of Jesus for our endemic racism. Lord, have mercy.

God's love embraces every nation; his authority is asserted over every race. The great commission which issues from this love for the world and from his authority over all the earth is to make every race 'learners of Christ'. That is the force of the imperative to 'make disciples'. It is less imperious and more suggestive of the humility with which Christ preached and lived the gospel. We are forever learners of Christ. None of us has arrived. We are always learning what it means to follow Christ. There's a cartoon of a confirmation service: the candidate kneeling before the bishop has an 'L' plate pinned to his back; it points up the truth that the newly confirmed Christian has not arrived but only just begun his journey of following Christ; as you look more closely at the bishop you see that woven into his mitre is also the letter 'L'; he too is learning what it means to see Christ in others and to be Christ to others.

Although we must distance the Church from the imperial image of lording it over other faiths and we would wish to colour in heavily the picture of the Church as a servant community in the world, the imperative remains not only in this text but throughout the Gospels that people of other races are also called to be learners of Christ. This will involve us in 'going . . . baptizing . . . and teaching . . .' This is one of the central issues facing the Church today: do we in the multi-faith global village have the right to make disciples of other races?

In his enthronement sermon the present Archbishop of Canterbury raised the issue when he welcomed to the cathedral leaders of other faith communities who are unable to accept all or most of the doctrines of the Church. As the Archbishop recognized, there are people of good will who share with Christians the same commitment to justice and mercy, to peace and freedom.

> You are also welcome today and by being here address an important question to those of us who follow Christ. You might put it to us in this form: 'We recognize that we live in a land that is Christian by heritage and predominant culture. But do we have a place with you?' Part of the answer lies in that shared texture of life I have just described. But deeper than that is the issue of integrity as persons and believers. I would want to put it this way: 'The faith that I have in Christ and his good name is so important that I am compelled – necessity is laid upon me – to share it with all people. But I trust I can listen to your story and respect your integrity even though having listened I may still want to offer to you, as to all, the claims of my Lord.' Through such listening, sensitive dialogue and mutual sharing I believe that our Church may

express its faith, whilst always learning from the very breadth of the nation we serve more of its full meaning.

In his sermon the Archbishop trod down some nettles and opened up a path through the woods. The inter-faith debate has often been polarized between those who advocate dialogue and those who insist on proclamation.

Those in favour of dialogue point up the humility of Christ and the need to respect the faith of others, especially of those who constitute a minority in the community; they emphasize the value of listening to the faith-stories of others and of accepting the integrity of other religious experiences; they argue that God reveals himself in many ways – in creation, in history, in Jesus – and that we must allow for the possibility of God revealing himself and unfolding his purposes in those beyond the Jewish and Christian communities, such as Cyrus in the Old Testament.

Those in favour of proclamation see that the earliest and most primitive strands of the gospel tell of Jesus preaching the Good News of the kingdom and challenging people's wills to a point of commitment and conversion; they argue that they have no desire to belittle the faith of others but that to deny the imperative to make disciples runs counter to the essence of the Christian faith and to the ethos of the New Testament Church; they insist that the world in which the early Church was immersed was as culturally and as religiously diverse as today's world but that this did not deflect the early Christians from the great commission.

The appeal of the Archbishop's sermon lies in its affirmation of both these polarized positions. What he does, in effect, is to move us away from the polarization of proclamation versus dialogue, and to offer a new way toward *proclamation in the context of dialogue*. This means working with people of other faiths, listening to their religious experiences and respecting their outlook; it means speaking with integrity of one's own experience of God and of the claims that Christ has laid upon

one's life. Proclamation in the context of dialogue is the pattern
that St Paul adopted in his mission to Athens in Acts 17:

> From one man he made every nation of men, that they should
> inhabit the whole earth; and he determined the times set for
> them and the exact places where they should live. God did
> this so that men would seek him and perhaps reach out for
> him and find him, though he is not far from each one of us.
> 'For in him we live and move and have our being.' As some
> of your own poets have said, 'We are his offspring.' (Acts
> 17:26–28)

'For in him we live and move and have our being' (17:28) is a
beautiful statement of faith about the universal embrace of
God. But it comes from neither a Jewish nor a Christian source.
Paul quotes approvingly from the Stoics. According to F. F.
Bruce in his commentary on the Greek text:

> The language here is quoted from an address to Zeus by his
> son Minos: They fashioned a tomb for them O holy and high –
> the Cretans, always liars, evil beasts, slow bellies. But thou art
> not dead; thou art risen and live for ever, for in thee we live
> and move and have our being.[2]

(N.B. Paul further quotes from this text in Titus 1:12 when he
describes the Cretans as 'liars'.) What is striking in this reference to Zeus is the resonance of the resurrection of Jesus which
Paul goes on to proclaim (17:31). What is significant is that Paul
identified the God and Father of our Lord Jesus Christ with the
description of Zeus.

In this episode Paul according to Bruce: 'consistently endeav-
ours to have as much common ground as possible with his audiences'. He quotes from their scriptures and displays an
understanding of their religious outlook. In doing so he established a dialogue in the context of which he goes on to testify to

the fuller revelation of God in the raising of Jesus Christ from the dead.

It has been pointed out that the response to Paul's message was very poor with only a few people becoming followers. But truth, especially in the history of Christianity, has never been determined by a majority verdict. The point of this passage in Acts is that the principal runner who carried the torch of the gospel, who called a spade a spade and anathematized heretics, found nothing compromising in entering into dialogue with another faith community. Yet clearly for Paul his mission involved more than dialogue. Necessity was laid upon him not only to listen but also 'to preach the gospel' . . . because it is the power of God for the salvation of everyone who believes; first for the Jew, then for the Gentile (Romans 1:16).

It is the uniqueness of Jesus and his authority in heaven and over the earth that compelled Paul to go and preach and which continues to inspire the mission of the Church. 'As the Father has *sent* me so am I *sending* you.' The implication of that sending is 'to make disciples' and we do that by 'going . . . baptizing . . . teaching . . .' We do that with humility and sensitivity but with the consciousness that the authority to do it stems from heaven itself.

The unique absolution of sins by Jesus Christ assures the Christian here and now of salvation. This is God's gift for the whole world. Through that forgiveness the believer enters a new relationship with God. God is no longer remote but intimately known as the good Father who forgives, provides for and protects his children. The consciousness that God is our good Father is instilled in us by the Spirit of God who inspires us to pray sometimes the briefest of prayers: 'Abba, Dear Father.' And so those who live under the authority of Jesus Christ baptize other learners of Christ in the name of the Father and of the Son and of the Holy Spirit. Being at one with the Father through the forgiveness of his son Jesus Christ and under the influence of his Holy Spirit is the definitive Christian experience into which all learners of Christ from every race were brought and baptized.

The initiative lies with God. He put it into the hearts of men and women of every race that they should 'seek him and perhaps reach out for him and find him, though he is not far from each one of us' (Acts 17:27). But he himself has more than matched that seeking, reaching out and finding by making himself visible, tangible and accessible. He has revealed himself. So, to return to the door through which we entered at the outset of this book, he does not leave us simply to discover what we can about ourselves, the world and God. As befits the God of love he discloses himself and reveals himself in the flesh and blood of Jesus of Nazareth. Yet it is more than a mission of divine disclosure. It is a mission of mercy in which God through his son Jesus Christ rescues us who from birth are hostages to sin, evil and death. The pledge to rescue is limited not to the Jews and Christians. The God without frontiers makes his appeal to every race. 'The promise is for you and your children and for all who are far off – for all whom the Lord our God will call' (Acts 2:39). It is a call that goes out to the ends of the earth, to every race under the sun, to every creature fashioned in the image of God. It is the gospel call: 'Repent and be baptized, every one of you, in the name of Jesus Christ so that your sins may be forgiven. And you will receive the gift of the Holy Spirit' (Acts 2:38).

Notes

1 Jesus, The Character of God

1   See Keith Ward, *A Vision to Pursue*.
2   Baillie, John, in *The Idea of Revelation in Recent Thought*.
3   Bruce, F. F., in *Epistle to the Hebrews*, p. 4.
4   Caird, G. B., in *Language and Imagery of the Bible*.
5   Avis, Paul, in *Authority, Leadership and Conflict in the Church*.

2 The Authority of Jesus to Judge

1   Wolterstorff, Nicholas, in *Lament for a Son*.

4 The Authority of Jesus to Lay Down His Life

1   Jeremias, J., in *The Parables of Jesus*, p. 132.
2   McQuarrie, J., in *Jesus Christ in Modern Thought*, p. 393.
3   *Servant* (DLT 1988).
4   Vanstone, W. H., in his beautiful book *The Stature of Waiting*.
5   Avis, Paul, in his stimulating book, *Authority, Leadership and Conflict in the Church*.

5 *The Authority of Jesus to Take Up His Life*

1. Norris, R. A., in *God and World in Early Christian Theology.*
2. Plato, *The Apology of Socrates.*
3. Plato, *The Republic.*
4. Weham, John, in *Easter Enigma* (Paternoster Press).
5. At Caster Conference 1992.

6 *The Authority of Jesus Over Evil*

1. Twelvetree, Graham, in his excellent book *Christ Triumphant: Exorcism Then and Now.*

7 *The Authority of Jesus to Heal*

1. Schillebeeckx, Edward, in *Jesus in our Western Culture* (SCM Press).
2. *Ibid.*
3. *Ibid.*, p. 20.

8 *The Authority of Jesus to Give Life*

1. Bishop John Taylor, *A Matter of Life and Death* (SCM Press).
2. *Ibid.*, p. 36.
3. Clark, Kenneth, in his autobiography *The Other Half* (Hamish Hamilton), p. 108.

9 *The Authority of Jesus to Teach*

1. Bailey, Kenneth, *Poet and Peasant* (Eerdmans).
2. McQuarrie, John, in *In Search of Deity: An Essay in Dialectical Theism.*
3. *Ibid.*

4   McIntyre, John, in his stimulating book *Faith, Theology and Imagination* (The Handsel Press).

5   *Ibid.*, p. 8.

6   Caird, G. B., in *The Language and Imagery of the Bible* (Duckworth), p. 2.

7   Orwell, George, in *Inside the Whale* (Penguin).

8   *Ibid*.

9   Dahl, Roald, *The Times*, 8–7–89.

10   *The Authority of Jesus to Make Disciples*

1   *Falling into Grace* (DLT).

2   Bruce, F. F., in *The Acts of the Apostles* (Tyndale), p. 338.